Blessed "Pests" of the Beloved West

An Affectionate Collection on Insects and Their Kin

Edited by
Yvette A. Schnoeker-Shorb
and
Terril L. Shorb

NATIVE WEST PRESS

A Native West Press Book
October 2003

Editors: Yvette A. Schnoeker-Shorb and Terril L. Shorb
Associate Editors: Cheryl A. Casey and Melanie R. Lefever
Assistant Reader: Albert F. Zalfini
Book and Cover Design by Amanda Summers
Cover Art by Edie Dillon
Cover Photography by Terril L. Shorb and Matt Welter
Inside Photography by Terril L. Shorb, Matt Welter, and Steve Prchal
Inside Art by Ellen Greenblum, Beth Neely, Don Rantz,
    Mara Trushell, and Nichole Trushell
Editorial Support: Ann J. Atchison
Consulting Research Librarian: Linda Butterworth
Consulting Catalog Librarian: Kay Lauster
Website Design by Derek Collins
Technical Support: Steve Barber
Printed by EMI Printworks

We gratefully acknowledge that "Bugs and Dread" as it appears in this collection is adapted
from *Kinship to Mastery: Biophilia in Human Evolution and Development* by Stephen R. Kellert.
Copyright © 1997 Stephen R. Kellert. Reprinted by arrangement with the author and
Island Press/Shearwater Books.

LCCN: 2002115077
Blessed "pests" of the beloved west: an affectionate collection on insects and their kin / edited
by Yvette A. Schnoeker-Shorb and Terril L. Shorb
    p. cm.
ISBN 0-9653849-3-4
        1. Insects—West (U.S.). 2. Insects—Literary collections. 3. Human-animal relationships.
        4. Insect pests—United States. 5. Insects—Ecology. I. Title
QL475.W3 B44 2003   595.7 BLE

For further information, please contact the publisher:

Native West Press
P.O. Box 12227, Prescott, AZ 86304
nativewestpres@cableone.net
www.nativewestpress.com

Manufactured in the United States of America
♲ Printed on recycled paper

With affection
for the awe-inspiring L.B.
who suggested the concept for this book. Be assured
we do know that a life-form's natural existence
precedes human temptation to classify it and that,
while conflicts (real or perceived) may occur, a species'
purpose on this Earth—whether deemed a mystery or
a mistake—cannot be judged as such by only one
other species.

Acknowledgments

We are profoundly appreciative of those many authors and poets within this collection who provided advice, emotional and intellectual support (including occasional doses of philosophical banter), encouragement, and spiritual inspiration during this book's development from the title-conception stage through its editorial journey into production and the creative hands of our trusted designer and friend, Amanda Summers, who has been part of Native West Press since its beginning in 1996.

We remember with love and gratitude the late Molly Zamore, altruist and guardian angel who provided partial funding for this project.

We extend many thanks to Carl Olson, associate curator in the University of Arizona Department of Entomology, for his saintly patience in regard to our consulting him, as well as for his good-natured and informed responses to our various questions ranging from the technical to the ethical.

We are immensely thankful to social ecologist and author Stephen R. Kellert, whose dedicated work of helping people to understand, maintain, and restore healthy relationships with nature has inspired the respective directions of our own lifework, and to his publisher, Island Press/Shearwater Books, for permission to include within this collection "Bugs and Dread," an adaptation from his book *Kinship to Mastery: Biophilia in Human Evolution and Development.*

We thank Mike Tribby, senior cataloger at Quality Books Inc., for his generosity in sharing with us preliminary, general knowledge of cataloging-in-publication information related to this book.

We acknowledge with fondness a sincere appreciation for our devoted and adventurous co-photographer, Matt Welter, one of whose notes to us reads as follows: "I must tell you that I did everything to get a tick this weekend. Walking through grassy fields, going bushwhacking, wearing light-colored pants. Nothing."

And finally, but definitely not least, we are extremely grateful to our contributing artists and photographers for endowing this book with their original works—and upon request at such short notice. We offer to these wonderfully creative people a very special thanks. Their works have graced specific pages of this book as follows:

Front Cover: "Grasshopper" by Edie Dillon
Front Cover: "Centipede" by Matt Welter
Title Page and Page 37: "Beetle on Grid" by Matt Welter
Page 17: "Mosquito" by Matt Welter
Page 20: "Bald-faced Hornet" by Matt Welter
Page 55: *Papilio multicaudata* by Nichole Trushell of
    the Highlands Center for Natural History
Page 63: "Wasp" by Ellen Greenblum
Page 64: "Ant" by Ellen Greenblum
Page 75 and 78: "Robber Fly" by Nichole Trushell
Page 81: "Fly with Shoes" by Matt Welter
Page 89: "Kissing Bug" by Mara Trushell (as rendered
    from a photo, courtesy of Dr. Michael J. Schumacher
    of the University of Arizona Health Sciences Center)
Page 105: "Tick" by Matt Welter
Page 107: "Millipede" by Matt Welter
Page 110: "Vinegaroon" by Steve Prchal of the Sonoran
    Arthropod Studies Institute
Page 121: "Bugs on Cup" by Beth Neely and Don Rantz
Page 123: "Bugs with Adobe" by Beth Neely and
    Don Rantz

The photograph "Family on Tractor" on Page 28 was taken circa 1949 by Madge Shorb.

Contents

Introduction

This is not a cute book. If sweet stories and poems about cuddling with caterpillars, flirting with flies, and talking with ticks were expected, we apologize for our title being misleading. Rather, this is an adventurous book, and the reader is invited to come along on an unusual exploration. Within these pages are the works of people from many different fields of expertise; these writers and poets are the guides for this journey. Many of the authors within this collection have had *intimate* experiences, not always intentionally, with some of our least loved, little, *pesky* participants in this strange and mysterious condition we all share called life. Other members of this book community offer unique and beneficial perspectives in regard to understanding human conflicts with some of these notorious creatures who dwell within the western half of the United States. The life-forms addressed within this book (many of whom have counterparts in the eastern U.S., as well as in other parts of the world) share in common that they are all endowed by our Western culture with the reputation of being, in one way or another, *pests*.

But, first, we come to a not so minor semantic issue: What is a *pest*? And by whom and how are *pest* species defined? Most of us would agree on certain capabilities with which a *pest* insect or other arthropod is endowed. Some of these endowments of pesky insects, arachnids, and other invertebrate kin are the abilities to impact humans in negative ways ranging from plague and disease, to crop destruction and economic hardship, to personal injury, to annoyance. One association of the word *pest* found in *The Oxford English Dictionary* suggests the capability of corrupting the air. However, we now arrive at an interesting challenge: When we consider *Homo sapiens*, we find that our own species shares analogously most of these pest-like attributes.

Let us consider, for instance, our impact on our own kind. We have the potential to cause widespread disease and death by having created biological weapons. In addition, through our massive processes of urban development and monocropping practices, we have impacted the balance of Earth's natural economy, thereby placing an inevitable hardship on ourselves, as well as on countless nonhuman affiliates.

Furthermore, in an attempt to keep this planetary garden livable for all six billion of us humans, we have now become reliant on our ever-changing technologies to remedy our injurious effects on an originally Earth-endowed balance within natural biodiversity. And, in regard to our own intra-species diversity, while we are making progress toward understanding the many variations of ourselves, intercultural tolerance is often interrupted by far more than mere annoyance with each other, often leading to large-scale irruptions of such maliciousness that actual body counts defy us. Finally, the Earth itself has suggested—in the form of the Larsen B ice shelf breaking off from Antarctica—that our pollution of the atmosphere has contributed more than we care to admit to global warming. Thus, our own species appears to meet all of the criteria to qualify *Homo sapiens* as a *pest* to itself. But we would be most unkind to define humans as such.

Nonetheless, because this book is particularly about *pests* of the American West, and the editors of this collection are both from the western United States and of the species *Homo sapiens*, we must admit to a slight tinge of embarrassment. However, we suspect that most humans, ourselves included, would take offense were the word *pest* used *seriously* in reference to our own kind—particularly given the implication of consequences once this general judgment has been made. The folly of such a designation would become quickly apparent to anyone cradling within his or her arms and making eye contact with a newborn member of our species. Instincts would override our intellectual ideologies because our instincts function to serve the survival of our species. There is within our genes a reason why most humans instinctually find appealing (and cute) certain features such as big, front-facing eyes, small noses, large foreheads, and awkward limb movements that suggest vulnerability. While the arthropods and other creatures represented within this collection obviously do not share these particular features, insects and their kin do share with humans the instinct to survive—indeed, for their species to survive, for this is the common denominator of all life.

Unfortunately, instincts of different life-forms may lead to respective survival strategies that result in conflicts. Humans tend to take this personally. It appears to be our human nature to do so, particularly if we feel that our ability or that of our loved ones to survive is threatened. We are not different from any other species, including those we collectively and commonly consider to be pests, in doing what we need to in order to accommodate our innate need to survive.

Thus it is not the intention of this book or of its authors and poets to deny that conflicts between humans and some insects, as well as their kin species, do occur. While many of these conflicts exist as fearful projections born in the human mind, real conflicts do exist between our own kind and certain life-forms. For instance, and typically beyond the American West, these conflicts can lead to serious consequences for humans, as in the case of a particular kissing bug who takes blood from the face and leaves microorganisms responsible for the fatal Chagas disease—a fact which one of the world's strongest activists for biodiversity refers to as "history's most unfair exchange." But humans are not always in the role as victims in these interspecific conflicts.

In general, and at the global level, relatively recent history has shown that when a species' existence conflicts with human interests, the other-than-human species has tended to come out on the losing end of the conflict. It is estimated by some scientific sources that human activities are causing extinctions of land species globally at a rate of one hundred to a thousand times faster than before our species came along. Furthermore, some ecologists inform that the projected rate of invertebrate extinctions alone, including insects and their kin, is conservatively estimated at a loss of

10,000 species annually. Indeed, conflicts between humans and these species do exist. But who precisely the *pest* is remains arbitrary.

Because we are human, our inclinations pull us over to the non-pest side of conflicts, from where we present this question: Should all the little beasts included in our societal spectrum of alleged pests still be considered such if these insects and their kin are not in conflict with humans or human enterprise? Certainly our industrialized media seem to suggest so. Considering the natural fear and dislike that many people have of particular insects, spiders, and other invertebrates, some corporate advertising messages appear to link perpetuation of these creatures' reputations as pests to profit. What is not told, of course, within the story lines of these types of advertisements (and similar to many plots of horror/science fiction movies and sensationalistic articles in tabloids) is that many insects, spiders, and earthworms are our beneficial associates and indispensable keepers of natural balance. And we also might be wise to ask this: When human activities have sacrificed the balance of Earth's natural ecosystems, thus causing conflicts among us and other species, should these species be considered pests? Or do these newly occurring conflicts serve as indicators that we need to become more mindful of the consequences of our enterprises?

Sometimes it is in our fear and frustration, rather than out of necessity, that we are most inclined to overlook life—little lives who, while unaware of us, just plead by their presence simply to be. Additionally, when real conflicts do arise, perhaps we are in such a hurry to extinguish the little beasts who have trespassed on us in ways that range from annoying to devastating that we fail to realize their activities are not the result of the "humanified" form of maliciousness we might attribute to them. And, finally, when we are forced into conflict by circumstances and feel we have no alternative but to intentionally end the existence of others, is being mindful not the least we can do to affirm our respect for life?

An entomologist once said to us, "It's hard not to feel lonely knowing you love creatures whom much of humankind loathes." We believe there is a place in our deeper humanity from which to generate a greater tolerance for insects and their kin.

The authors within this collection have in common an affection for life and a respect for *natural* biodiversity—and Earth's millions of years experience at balancing it. These writers and poets represent a diversity of disciplines from within the sciences, social sciences, arts, and education, and their contributions reflect a broad spectrum of approaches to understanding human relationships with some of our most disliked, little affiliates. These essays and poems serve to inspire mindfulness even when complexity and circumstances prevent solutions from being ideal. Ranging from the cautious to the humorous, the disturbing to the comforting, the informative to the imaginative, the expected to the surprising, the works within these pages offer some welcome doses of perspective related to a variety of insects and their kin who dwell within or whose regions extend to the American West. While these small creatures of occasional conflict may be deemed *pests* by our culture, they are, like all of us, members of the extended family of life that is Nature's true blessing.

Yvette A. Schnoeker-Shorb and Terril L. Shorb
19 September 2003

In Order
That We
Understand

Insects

PHILIP MILLER

Look how closely they stick to us,
whining at our noses,
buzzing at our toes, ready to impose
themselves upon our briefest
exposure of flesh or sweat:
those striped bees whose very breath hums
underneath our breath or a tiny, delicate
mosquito droning in our ear loud enough
to wake us, longing for our warm
red type O or A or B,
plus or minus.
It could care less; it sucks—as do the flea,
bed bug, and gnat
with appendages and pressure
the weight of a fly's
wing, a gnat's eyebrow, but stings hot and sharp
enough to penetrate tough skin, to make
us yelp or dance or slap our foreheads, just missing
the whizzing creature, the scarlet welt
rising, like the hives and rashes,
the poisoned knots
from slender, handsome wasps
of ivory, jet, or Chinese red,
of the purple-banded hornet, the cow killer,
velvet black and vermilion, or the ordinary acid-tailed
ant, the blue bottle fly—also in green and liquid gold—
all these intense, soft engines
capable of a nibble without which the insect and the human
might never really meet, and we might not understand

the great need of these smallest animals for us,
their bites so much bigger than their buzzes or bulks,
these minute twinges serving to remind us
of our final surrender to the carrions and dungs
bright beetles, round scarabs, gaudy royal blues
and ruby reds, so many interested bugs
who love us alive and even after death
turning their black bead-like eyes
toward us, fanning us with humming wings,
twitching an alert antenna,
opening sharp jaws,
waving a horned and antlered beak.

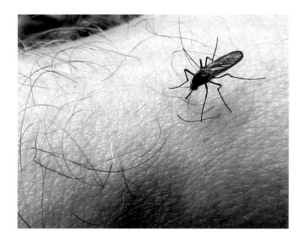

Bugs and Dread

STEPHEN R. KELLERT

Editors' Note: The following first appeared in its original version as "Bugs, Rats, and Dread" within the chapter "Of Fear and Loathing" in *Kinship to Mastery: Biophilia in Human Evolution and Development* by Stephen R. Kellert. Copyright © 1997 Stephen R. Kellert. This modified version is adapted and reprinted here by arrangement with the author and Island Press/Shearwater Books.

Anxiety, fear, and sometimes terror are still part of our relationship with the natural world. Particular environmental features and events elicit fear and avoidance under widely varying circumstance with little provocation. Although our fears and anxieties may be out of proportion to the actual risks involved, the inclination to avoid certain creatures and landscapes is motivated by more than careful calculation alone. We seem predisposed to evade certain features of the natural world almost independent of their immediate and obvious danger.

Distancing oneself from certain creatures and landscapes does not necessarily produce intense fear or dislike. Insulating oneself from threatening objects by minimizing, repressing, or denying their relevance or even existence can sometimes accomplish the same purpose. Often we practice "out of sight, out of mind" as a way of coping with anxiety and threat. Modern urbanization and separation from nature make this kind of apathy all too easy to achieve.

Many insects and spiders provoke fears and antipathy. In a study I conducted with colleagues, we examined attitudes toward insects, spiders, and other invertebrates among the general public, farmers, scientists, and environmental organization members.* The great majority of respondents, with the exception of scientists, expressed strong dislike of bugs, beetles, ants, crabs, ticks, cockroaches, and especially biting and stinging invertebrates such as wasps, spiders, mosquitoes, and scorpions. Indeed, a majority of the general public indicated a willingness to eliminate mosquitoes, cockroaches, fleas, moths, and spiders altogether. Invertebrates were generally viewed as mindless; incapable of emotion and rational decision making; and possessing little ethical, ecological, or practical value.

What accounts for the widespread aversion, anxiety, and hostility toward many invertebrates, especially insects? Why do so many people lack awareness or appreciation of the various ecological, scientific, and utilitarian benefits of these creatures? Why do certain invertebrates provoke a willingness to exterminate them altogether?

Antipathy toward invertebrates often originates in the association of these animals with agricultural destruction and disease. Destroying invertebrates has been linked to protecting crops and preventing illness. Producing food surpluses has been achieved by creating vast monocultures and eliminating insect "pests," often through the widespread use of toxics and biocides. The availability of inexpensive and plentiful food has been partly a result of our unrelenting "war on bugs."

Notions of disease transmission and prevention similarly focus on the danger of various invertebrates and other microorganisms. Mosquitoes are associated with malaria, fleas with plague, ticks with fever, worms with intestinal problems, cockroaches with hygiene-related diseases, and so on. Entire medical specialties like parasitology have been built around the role of insects and other invertebrates as vectors of disease. To many people, these organisms intimate illness and disorder. Frequently they are victims of guilt by association.

Human antipathy toward invertebrates sometimes extends

beyond the rational to levels of extreme fantasy and antago-
nistic projection. What other attributes do these creatures
possess that elicit such hateful
feelings? Perhaps people feel
threatened by the radically
different biological and
behavioral characteristics

and survival strategies of these creatures. Insects and other
invertebrates strike many of us as otherworldly and bizarre.
They possess too many legs, move in odd and disturbing
ways, boast strange and bewildering body shapes, typically
come in small, even microscopic, packages. They can also
reproduce in staggering numbers in a remarkably short
period of time.

Insects, spiders, and other invertebrates often defy
human notions of normality. They stretch our empathetic
capacity and acceptance. Perhaps most disturbing, these
creatures appear to lack a mental life: they reveal neither
humanlike emotions of warmth and affection nor the intellectual characteristics of rationality and choice. The mind
and soul appear irrelevant to their existence. Sometimes the
peculiarities of invertebrates strike us as strange and exotic,
the source of great mystery and curiosity. More often, they
provoke the inclination to dislike the grotesque, fear the
monstrous, and reject the alien and incomprehensible.

The psychologist James Hillman has suggested that
invertebrates threaten our cherished assumptions of indi-
viduality, selfhood, and identity. The enormous numbers
of invertebrates imply the insignificance of the individual;
the seeming absence of mental life implies the irrelevance
of personal consciousness. The sanctity of a single human
life appears threatened by the idea that a single bee hive
contains tens of thousands of organisms, a single ant colony

hundreds of thousands, or that the number of beetle species numbers in the millions.

Invertebrates lack the characteristics most people associate with moral standing: feelings, autonomy, rationality, choice, ethical responsibility. These creatures seem to respond only to the dictates of a rigid genetics, forsaking all selfhood for the sake of the species. Appearing mindless, lacking emotion and intellect, they emerge as symbols of madness and irrationality.

Invertebrates threaten by being so indifferent to our desires and presumptions of importance. Our homes, offices, buildings, even hospitals, are routinely invaded by insects and spiders, defying our notions of human sanctity and omnipotence. Most mammals, birds, and other vertebrates flee from human presence; insects and spiders frequently seem unaware, possibly disdainful, of our existence. They live in our homes and workplaces, and we cringe at hearing that seldom in our lives will we be more than five feet from a spider.

* Stephen R. Kellert, "Values and Perceptions of Invertebrates," *Conservation Biology* 7 (1993): 845-855.

House Cleansing

CAROL N. KANTER

Some years I battle ants. Who knows
how they get in? But whole battalions
infiltrate, commandeer
my house, troop anywhere
they please between my Raid attacks.

Other years my in-house wars
rage against mosquitoes, flies,
each spider, smaller moths,
the odd milli- or centipede,
and always anything that smacks

of roach. But my crickets play
in the basement undisturbed.
And when ladybugs want in—
cling six feet strong to screen doors
until their soft slow wings whirr

them up to appliqué my ceiling
with polka dots on grounds of red
or last year's subtle amber tone—
lest they feel too much at home,
I wish them back outside, not dead,

and go to lengths to turn them out,
as I would any butterfly
or larger moth, daddy-longlegs,
caterpillars, and sometimes worms,
hornets, bumble bees and wasps.

But what's this on my kitchen floor?
A spider—mutant of Poe's Gold Bug,
its shiny metal carapace
shrunk to encase a tiny head.
It glints here in the morning sun

like a bronzed avatar. I offer
her a lift on my legal pad.
Outside, I blow hard to fly
her off. But she knows her own mind
and quick as you please she spins a line,

fastens the loose end up top
and with grace drops straight down,
leaving me alone
to plumb
how I discriminate with bugs.

Spring Migration

MARGARITA ENGLE

once again
just as promised
the blessed season of ants and millipedes
has arrived
  armies of beetles and moths seize our winter-weary house
  turning the walls inside-out

suddenly
everything that has been musty and stale
spills outdoors
over these inverted walls
people, books, papers, pencils, all is flowing
riparian and leafy-green
  sliding down vertical cliffs
    of dusty brick and cobwebbed stucco

this is the season
when small creatures
rush indoors to replace us
patrolling the couch and dinner table
claiming their ancestral territory
while we
moved by the same heat of restless wonder
flow outward
to take our rightful place
as wandering nomads

The Little People of the Green Things

JOANNE E. LAUCK

Each spring I wait for the aphids to appear on the two rose bushes next to my cottage. They seem to arrive mysteriously overnight. One day the rose bushes are bare, and the next day there are literally hundreds of these insects coating the buds and stems. Aphids are also called plant lice. I call them "the little people of the green things," following the example of an imaginative writer who penned an article about them in the late 1920s. The arrival of the little people is one of the events, like the appearance of mourning cloak butterflies in the sky and the pale green lacewings dancing around my porch light, that marks the coming of warm weather.

Typically these creatures have been looked on as vermin who suck the life out of their green hosts, plunging their beaks into the "helpless" plants to feed. Articles on garden pests usually describe them as heartless automatons who don't care that the ailing, blighted plants are powerless and at their mercy. I wonder, though, how accurate this portrayal of their relationship is. For one thing, plants aren't victims of whoever comes along. They can resort to any number of devices to make their collective will known in a given situation. A case in point are the plants who respond to the over-zealous nibbling of foraging insects by producing a chemical that either gives the bugs indigestion or makes them feel falsely sated. And an injured leaf can release jasmonic acid to signal other leaves on its green network to bolster their chemical defenses before the bugs arrive.

Because these chemical actions and reactions happen

underneath our human senses, we can't easily determine the nature of the interaction between a given plant and the insects on and about it. Our assumptions therefore color our observations. If we assume, for example, that only competition and struggle drive the interchange, a guiding assumption for a long time, we are likely to interpret what we see only in these terms. Yet, evidence is mounting for an entirely different view of how the world works. It is a view that fits inside me easily in a way that the traditional view never did. This new hypothesis, proposed by leading microbiologist Lynn Margulis, sees life as having evolved from networking, cooperation, and dynamic connectedness.

Perhaps if we knew the depth and breadth of the bond between plants and insects we would understand why plants and insects resist our best attempts to separate them. It would explain, for instance, why we fight an uphill battle when we welcome house and garden plants and try to bar their multi-legged companions. We can't even eat greens without eating insects—including whole insects, body parts and eggs—because farmers can't separate them from the harvested plant.

I think it likely that plants and insects participate in as many different kinds of relationships as do people. Many plants use insect allies to keep marauding insects in check, much as we do when we call on friends to help us dissuade unwanted attention. Corn and bean plants emit a chemical scent to summon parasitic wasps to help them when certain kinds of caterpillars nibble at their leaves. Answering the call, the wasps lay eggs in the caterpillars. When the rapidly developing larvae hatch, they feed on their caterpillar hosts, effectively checking the population.

Still other plants coax ants to stay close to them so that these fierce warriors will discourage other insects from feasting on them. To make themselves attractive to the ants, they secrete a solution rich in sugars and amino acids. And it works. The ants love it and don't stray far.

Relationships that are obviously beneficial to both insect

and plant abound in nature. Western scientists call them symbiotic relationships emphasizing the survival benefits they bring to those involved. I prefer the way indigenous people describe them: as bound by bonds of friendship and kinship.

Our specialists don't lack for information about symbiotic relationships, but neither expert nor layperson holds dear what is known. That seems to be the problem. We simply don't hold insects or plants dear. We don't allow our hearts and imaginations to interact with what we observe or the information we take in from reading or sitting in a lecture hall. Adopting the framework of traditional science doesn't help either. By reducing the alliances between insects and plants to a series of mutually self-serving activities, we place these relationships in a framework that is too small.

It has only been in recent years that we haven't been discouraged, ashamed even, or afraid of anthropomorphizing to translate the wealth of available facts about plants and animals into anything real and immediate. Yet personalizing what we observe allows us to relate to other species and activates our feeling connection to the world. And feelings empower facts, lending them the power to inform and

enrich our lives. We can understand symbiotic relationships because we have many of our own, and healthy relationships—the ones that are good for both parties—cross species lines.

The relationships between plants and insects that don't appear to be mutually beneficial, like the one between aphids and their green hosts, are less easily explained in relational terms. In most instances the insects seem to be overrunning the plants, taking advantage of the rootedness of their green benefactors. But is that the full story? I recently read that plants that endure an "attack" of caterpillar larvae have fewer problems with predators later and actually do better than those that are saved from the caterpillar's bite. So interaction with certain kinds of insects can make a plant strong and hardy.

We've been conditioned to think of many insects as adversaries because we are taught that commercial food crops are continually threatened by certain insects, which, in turn, forces our farmers to battle them with deadly chemicals. It is the official story. We are apt to believe it because we think of insects as untrustworthy members of the earth community, willing and able to overrun both plants and humans. But this belief arises from years of being bombarded by negative images of insects and living under the shadow of a general cultural condemnation of insects, a topic I have written about extensively. When we remember that much of what we know about plant-insect relationships comes from a science that focuses on the separateness of things and more often than not makes observations with the intent to control or eradicate the subjects, we entertain the first important seed of doubt.

That doubt led me to delve into the literature, looking for what really might be happening in our growing fields. I found a great deal of evidence that refutes the official story that insists we need to wage war against the insects to grow crops successfully. Many agricultural experts have demonstrated that in a balanced environment insects attack only weak and dying plants. As nature's disposal crew, insects are summoned when they are needed and repelled when they are not. And who summons them?—why the plants do. Insects communicate with plants (and with each other) using a variety of antennae tuned to the infrared band of the electromagnetic spectrum. By sensing radiation from oscillating molecules emitted by plants, they know when a plant is failing. And the sicker the plant, the more powerful the scent it emits, and the easier for the insect to home in on it.

In an unbalanced environment other forces also come into play—factors conveniently omitted from the official story. Consider that when a plant is not getting the nutrients it needs from the soil (and most current large-scale agricultural practices do not replenish the soil), it loses its vitality and is likely to call in insects to dismantle it. So the presence of large numbers of insects may be a message telling us the plant is sick. Their numbers might also be letting us know that the limits that operate in a natural system to keep all species in balance have been altered or eliminated. It's not news. We thought we could override natural systems and plant acres of single crops in order to realize greater yields. Armed with pesticides and now genetic modification techniques, we have been unwilling to sacrifice efficiency and quick profits for long-term sustainability. We have tried instead to fix all signs of imbalance by killing the messengers.

Since we fully believed we could replace natural systems with alien ones, the fact that many insects prefer only one plant, can multiply quickly given enough food, and mutate if threatened didn't seem important. It was important. The weevil, for instance is a specialist. This easily recognizable beetle, with its long, curved snout half the length of its body, only likes one food plant. In fact, each of the 40,000 some species likes a specific plant, and most common trees, shrubs, and green-leafed plants are host to one weevil species. The cotton boll weevil likes cotton. When we planted acre after acre of cotton, it multiplied according to its nature. How could it not? And how could we reasonably fault it for that? But the fields of cotton were not a gift from the beetle gods or homage from human beings in appreciation of the weevil. We had no intention of sharing our cotton with insects. Farmers, trying to protect their investment, sprayed the weevils with a variety of insecticides, determined to eradicate them. The applications of deadly chemicals only set the weevils back temporarily and actually served them over time because it killed their natural predators. The constant attacks also forced the cotton boll weevil and other insect species to change and adapt to survive. In turn we created more effective weapons, having created a real enemy out of a creature whose only fault was liking one kind of plant.

Not every farming community stayed on the battlefield. I like the story, though it occurred beyond the West, of how one county in Alabama surrendered to the cotton boll beetle. On the verge of bankruptcy, these farmers gave up their single-crop strategy with its government stipends, and they diversified. Imagine their surprise and happiness when they realized greater profits from planting a variety of crops than in their most plentiful years of cotton. And the best part of the story is that they acknowledged the wisdom of the cotton boll weevil and erected a statue in the center of the town to honor the insect for insisting that they keep the natural systems of their land intact.

When we garden, we would do well to remember the message of the boll weevil and uproot the assumptions the media have thrust upon us that divides all other species into good and bad based on whether they meet our short-term goals. We have all learned that the presence of an insect, other than a ladybug, on a flower or vegetable plant means trouble is brewing, and it is just a matter of time before the plant is overwhelmed. Last summer when a friend of mine took up organic gardening, she showed me a picture of a caterpillar that she had found on a parsley plant in her garden. Not wishing to harm it, she had plucked it off the plant and placed it on the trunk of a tree located a good distance from the garden. I questioned her: "You didn't have enough parsley to share with the caterpillar?" She looked at me blankly for a moment and then stammered, "Well, yes, I have a whole row, but I thought if there was one, there would be hundreds and they would take it all." As it was, unless the caterpillar had the strength to crawl all the way back to its food source or had already eaten enough to initiate its transformation into a butterfly, it probably died on the tree, and my friend lost a chance to help a yellow and black swallowtail butterfly emerge.

When insects appear to overwhelm a plant, their presence indicates one of two things: either a natural cycle of transformation and growth is at work, as when masses of a particular insect emerge at the beginning of a season, or a problem exists. Perhaps the plant is not receiving what it needs for its optimal growth, or there is an imbalance in the environment or in the human community. Whatever the problem, the insects are the messengers alerting them to it.

I check periodically on my roses to see how they and the aphids that visit them are faring. That is how I know that two or three weeks after the initial appearance of the little people of the green things, they disappear as mysteriously as they came. Perhaps they are all eaten by ladybugs (although if they are, it happens when I am not around). In the last couple of years, I've noticed that the little people only cover two or three buds and stems on each rose bush, and I worry about their decline. I reassure myself by thinking that maybe these visitors come not as a feast for ladybugs or to win the favor of the bees, ants, butterflies and flies that savor their honey-dew droppings, but to meet the human being who welcomes them. I must admit that they have grown dear to me.

There is a miniature world in our backyards that would

come alive and nourish us if we paid attention to it and learned who's who with a genuinely friendly and curious attitude. And if we knew what relationships—what bonds of friendship—existed between our plants and local insects, we could cherish them. Recognizing that all is well, we would neither bemoan the arrival of the little people of the green things nor fear their impact on our beloved plants. We would recognize love at work and look on fondly, noting a natural cycle in process and praising them both.

The Ecology of Sacred Spaces

JEFFREY A. LOCKWOOD

For a species to become wholly reliant on a place or a habitat requires that it sacrifice other options, accepting the risks of being profoundly and deeply linked to a landscape. When in the course of evolution such an ecological setting is found, the species comes to flourish in this place. The wintering grounds of monarch butterflies and the spawning grounds of salmon are such places in the modern world. The fertile river valleys of the western United States were such places for the Rocky Mountain locust—the creature that blackened the skies of the early pioneers, brought trains to a halt as the crushed bodies of the insects greased the rails, and represented what the United States government considered to be the single greatest impediment to the settlement of the West. When these lands were transformed by plows and cows, the refuge of the locust was destroyed and the living wildfires that once swept across the continent were extinguished. We have such a special place, a sociobiological habitat that comprises less than a millionth of the Earth's surface but through which 70% of the human species passes several times a year—our sacred spaces: churches, mosques, synagogues, and temples.

The concept of the sacred is rooted in the same etymological origin as is sacrifice, which is an act that engenders holiness through loss, suffering, denial, or pain. Holiness, in turn, is a condition associated with transcendent meaning, so that a place of sacrifice is imbued with importance greater than its physical context. So, in our places of worship we often relate stories of sacrifice. Conversely, places of momentous loss often become sacred, such as battlefields at Gettysburg and Little Big Horn, the Edmund Pettus Bridge in Selma, the North Bridge in Concord, or a simple roadside cross adorned with flowers. We also honor places of sanctuary where we have found safety amidst a world of turmoil and trouble, such as the hiding place of Anne Frank, Thoreau's cabin site at Walden Pond, or our childhood home. Our most sacred spaces both remind us of suffering and offer us sanctuary. But what of other species? Does sacrifice or sanctuary define the extraordinary places in their

lives? Do these places need to be consciously and intentionally chosen, or can a sacred space emerge in the context of
evolution and ecology?

We are reluctant to call the habitats of other species
sacred because their sacrifices are not volitional, and their
seeking of sanctuary seems unconscious. But we did not plan
for a grassy knoll in Dallas to be the place to lose President
Kennedy; we did not intend for a buck-and-rail fence east
of Laramie to be the site where Matthew Shepard would be
sacrificed to our fear of differences; and we did not design
the basements and attics of the houses along the underground railroad to be sanctuaries for runaway slaves. As
self-aware animals, we do what we can to honor and protect
our sacred spaces, and, perhaps, we should not deny other
creatures their own ways of knowing and keeping deeply valued places in so far as they are able. All species have stories
of suffering and sanctuary in ecological and evolutionary
time. To have arrived in this world is to have risked, lost,
groped, huddled, and grasped using those capacities that
one's form and function provided. These stories and places
of loss and triumph are encoded in all beings. Are they less
real or less important if they are not maintained by thought
or word?

The complex and intimate connections between the
land and native species are difficult—perhaps impossible—
to express in objective, scientific terms, but sacred places
are central to the well-being of many creatures. Even with
all of the "right" conditions of temperature, light, humidity,
and diet, animals often languish in zoos. They are unable to
express what is missing, and perhaps we would be unable to
understand, unless we too had experienced the soul-wrench-
ing loss of being forced from a farm or ranch that had been
in the family for generations or being driven from a home-
land that defined our traditions, stories, and hopes.

Orthoptera

Lepidoptera

Hymenoptera

On Insects
– In a Particular
Order

Diptera

Coleoptera

Other Orders

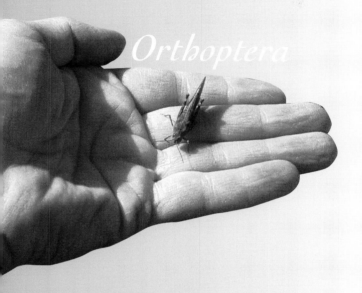

Orthoptera

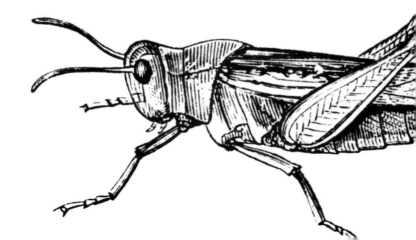

Variety and Black Grasshoppers

ELIZABETH BERNAYS

The midsummer sun bleaches the colors in the Arizona desert, and my eyes feel weak. It is noon, 105 degrees Fahrenheit in the shade; a grasshopper crawls up on the trunk of a mesquite tree and settles to rest among its foliage. It is a fine specimen, as large as a mouse and glossy black. Yellow marks trace the outline of a jacket on its thorax and on the helmet of its head, while its front wings have bright green veins. Its common name is the "horse lubber." I watch a large female. I have been watching her since 7:00 a.m., when she started her day. Plants rejected or accepted, times spent in each feeding bout, movements between plants—details fed into my hand-held computer. She has been on the move almost nonstop and has fed on fifty different plant types, challenging my attentiveness and endurance. As temperatures rose, her movements became faster, her feeding furious, but at last it was too hot. Needing to escape the fierce ground, she made for the breeze above in the mesquite tree. In a couple of hours she will descend, and I will continue my recording. I can predict this because for eleven days I have been standing out in the summer sun, watching individual lubbers for ten hours at a time.

In the heat of the afternoon I sometimes wonder why I do this. But I burn with curiosity about the behavior of these animals. I know that individual lubbers eat a wide variety of plant species, and it is an unusual strategy for plant-feeding insects.

Moving about, they expose themselves to discovery by predators—birds and lizards. Why do they march about eating so many different things? I watch and record; for ten hours each day I almost become a grasshopper.

Three months later, I have the field observations analyzed, and I have results from laboratory experiments. These big, shiny black creatures have a lifestyle as distinctive as their appearance. They have a preference for poisonous plants, disdaining blander foods. But given just one plant in captivity, they become sick. Eating many different plants, it turns out, prevents the level of a single plant chemical from reaching a poisonous dose, just as with people.

In addition to diluting potential toxins by wide-ranging foraging, horse lubbers absorb a variety of poisons out of plants and store them in special glands. If attacked, they lift black and green front wings, flash red back wings, buzz, and exude an ill-smelling, frothy, poisonous mixture. Predators spit them out and remember their unique sounds, smells, and sights. Broad eating habits enable the grasshopper to dilute toxins *and* sequester a mixture of nasty ones.

But how do they choose? They contain too many different plants to be able to associate the taste of any one plant with its value after eating it, so they cannot *learn* to choose well and avoid something that makes them sick. However, if given a synthetic food with a simple flavor—say, vanilla—they eat it for a few short bouts of feeding, then reject it. They readily accept the same food if the flavor is changed to, say, peppermint, but again, only for a few bouts. And after a while on peppermint, they again accept vanilla. In short, they eat and grow well on identical foods if new flavors are added at intervals. They choose novelty over sameness—variety, it turns out, is their spice of life, just as it is for me.

Unlike me, my partner likes consistency. Each morning when I get up I like to choose yogurt or fruit or egg or toast or any other thing for breakfast; and I *love* to choose. By contrast, he has cornflakes every morning, always. There are many people like me who love variety in everything; others are most comfortable with complete predictability. Why? Consistency needs less thought perhaps. Regular habits leave the mind free for other activities. If you like to have a choice, then you must choose and that can take time, sometimes long periods of dithering. But then again, does it matter?

I return to grasshoppers. The horse lubber has little to worry about with respect to predators. It can take its time, make choices. By contrast, many other insects are well camouflaged, wary, and feed on few plant types. They are acceptable to predators. So, on the one hand, become adapted to feed on one plant type and hide from predators; on the other hand, keep the opportunity of choosing the best food among a mixture and make itself chemically nasty.

People have alternatives too: Be a jack-of-all-trades and master of none, or be an expert at something. Each has value, depending upon the situation. Perhaps the commonest tradeoff is between doing a job slowly, carefully, and well, but making slow progress, versus doing the job fast and sloppily but getting a lot done. I might want the first approach in a nurse and the second in a house cleaner. Perhaps there was clearer biological significance of variation in our evolutionary past. Did novelty seekers find new food and tools while others kept strict attention to well-known paths and got routine jobs done? Perhaps today the inventors of computer programs are novelty seekers, and the consistent users of programs are the best at getting down to work. Psychologists tell us that novelty seekers are more likely to engage in dangerous activity—a risk. And some sociologists claim there is a relationship between some risk-taking behaviors and attractiveness to women—a benefit.

Afternoon came and indeed my lubber descended, shiny black and splendid with yellow braid on her uniform, to wander among the desert wildflowers, to eat here and there, to enjoy the smorgasbord. And at the end of the day I too sit and enjoy a meal of many different foods.

The Joy and Wonder of Fear and Loathing

JEFFREY A. LOCKWOOD

Within minutes, our hands are covered in feces and vomit. Our quarry, the Plains lubber grasshopper, is surely one of the most disgusting creatures to subdue. *Brachystola magna* is the largest of all insects on the Wyoming grasslands and is reminiscent of the chewed, cigar butts that I used to encounter jammed into ashtrays when I was a kid. They're about the same size and equally appealing. This is no dainty grasshopper capable of lithesome leaps—it has the heft of a breakfast sausage. Every summer we collect a few dozen prairie lubbers from the weedy roadsides in southeastern Wyoming.

The only way to gather these grasshoppers is by hand. An insect net is an effective means of capturing grass**hoppers** that are willing and able to live up to their names, but the net snares few of these lumbering creatures. They are clumsy behemoths, hopping with the agility of insectan sumo wres- tlers—hence their name "lubbers." Furthermore, these lubberly beasts are incapable of flight, having their wings reduced to stubby pads. As such, they are simple to grab. Or so it should seem.

Upon capture, their first and most revolting defensive strategy is to regurgitate copiously. Many species exhibit this defensive behavior, and as kids we referred to grasshoppers as "spitting tobacco juice." Indeed, the cola-colored fluid resembles the expectorant of tobacco chewers in its capacity to stain whatever it hits. Of course, the grasshoppers aren't spitting masticated wads of chewed tobacco. Rather, they are heaving up the contents of their foreguts (the anatomical equivalent of our stomachs) which consist of liquified sunflower leaves, their favorite food. The prairie lubber manages to produce this material in truly impressive quantities, smearing itself and its captor with the dark brown fluid. For this grasshopper, however, the effort to repulse its assailant is not complete.

The restrained grasshopper next begins to defecate prodigiously. As opposed to vomiting, this offensive approach to defense is not widely practiced among the lubber's brethren. Perhaps it wouldn't be particularly disgusting for most species, as grasshoppers generally produce very dry, compact fecal pellets the size of sesame seeds. The lubber, on the other hand, can produce a dozen, mouse-scaled, mushy turds in quick succession. Perhaps the sunflowers, being rather more succulent than prairie grasses, provide enough fluid to allow this grasshopper the luxury of softer excrement. Thus, an experienced collector avoids the rear end of the grasshopper and holds the insect at bay for a few seconds until it has exhausted its colonic arsenal. If one is too hasty in dropping the repulsive creatures into a collecting bag, the grasshoppers quickly foul the container with smeared feces, making any future handling a most unpleasant prospect.

These behaviors of the prairie lubber suggest a rather profound and profane form of interspecific communication. Vital information is transmitted between grasshoppers and other creatures—people in particular. It doesn't take Dr. Doolittle to decipher the meaning, but that is because the insect has translated the message into a language that we can readily comprehend—"Put me down!" Nature does not offer many opportunities for us to encounter a communique so explicitly intended for us and originating in the mind of a creature so different from us. This grasshopper has come to understand—at least in evolutionary terms, if not with regard to individual consciousness—what regurgitation and defecation mean to humans. Sometimes, I wonder if some of these creatures might even possess a vague sense of what they're telling me. There's always one or two who seem to engage in excretion with a perverse gusto beyond that required by strict necessity. Defecation with an exclamation mark of sorts.

The revulsion in handling these creatures is proportional to the assailant's capacity to experience disgust or at least to value cleanliness. And so, the message from the lubbers seems particularly—if not solely—tuned to our senses and sensibilities. Modern culture has crafted from our natural fastidiousness a variety of behaviors far more biologically inane than the spectacles that we deem absurd. The peacock might prance and the stag might have enormous antlers, but we have embedded antibiotics in our plastics, our meat, and our underwear. I would not be surprised if the anatomical models in biology labs will soon be molded from antibiotic plastics, completing our separation from the living world. It seems that we are genetically predisposed to avoid, or at least to easily learn to avoid, filth. And this is the visceral reaction that makes our encounter with the lubber grasshopper so compelling.

I've grown fond of grasshoppers in my fifteen years of working as an entomologist at the University of Wyoming. These are beautifully colored, elegantly sculpted, gracefully moving creatures, putting to scorn, as Walt Whitman said in *Leaves of Grass*, the most exquisite products of human engineering. But a conflict arises when I realize that these awesome creatures can be absolutely awful. In attempting to be tolerant, even accepting, of other life-forms, a kind of biopolitical correctness tends to sanitize gut feelings. My primal sense of loathing is dulled, which makes me a better neighbor for other people and species. However, when a humongous insect regurgitates and defecates (perhaps I should say "pukes and craps" to retain the earthy sense of these crude behaviors), no amount of cultivated sensitivity converts this from being a truly disgusting encounter. There is something true and meaningful about my instinctive reactions, and the grasshoppers allow—indeed force—me to honor these intuitions. The lubber grasshopper is being authentically gross because it intends to be. And it is in my genuine biological nature to honor their revolting efforts, to issue forth a guttural tribute to their nastiness, to twist my face into a mask of revulsion.

As a professor, I know that I must provide my students with authentic experiences, for these—not theories, principles, or techniques—are the lessons they will remember. All of my erudite lectures, red-scrawled corrections, and clever exams may help them learn the content of science. But the labors of the mind will only be valued, and the self-discipline of the scholar will only mature, if the students have a passion for their work. And passion can be evoked but never taught. So we visit the dusty roadsides of Wyoming in mid-summer to play under the formal guise of a collecting trip. Here is the chance to give my students a firsthand, utterly base encounter with a socially unfiltered and sublimely repulsive aspect of nature: lubber grasshoppers.

Although trained in the culture of science, the students approach the lubbers like kids who are simultaneously attracted to and repulsed by a run-over cat or a fresh cow pat. They might be efficiently educated via pinned insects in the museum or textbook descriptions of life histories, but these slow-moving, colorfully adorned, bald-headed, fat-bellied, Buddha-like grasshoppers remind us that the world must be encountered directly, on its own terms. Such simple and primal experiences reconnect professor and students to the living world. This messy, sloppy, slimy world engages the spirit of the child, the source of wonder without which science becomes as sterile as an antibiotic plastic model.

War Memorial

JEFFREY A. LOCKWOOD

The 3-year war for
the West was waged with
men, maps, planes, poisons against
grasshoppers.

To commemorate
nineteen-eighty-six:
"The Battle of Idaho."
Imagine—

The Battlefield:
Tract of desolate rangeland =
    9,375 square miles.
        To walk its border allow 24 days,
        To paint its interior give each US citizen 10 spray cans,
        To mow its surface hire everyone in New York City for a day,
        To see its area imagine 6 million football fields spread
            over the land.
        If you can.

The Weapon:
Malathion in drums =
    375,000 gallons.
        To spray it turn on your hose for 2 months,
        To store it in beer bottles line up a row 157 miles long,
        To share it with everyone in the US allow a heaping
            teaspoon each,
        To feel its weight imagine a grasshopper crushed under the
            mass of a human.
        If you can.

The Enemy:
Rangeland grasshoppers =
    726 trillion individuals.
        To store their bodies allot 250 gymnasiums,
        To distribute their remains give each person on Earth
            100 corpses,
        To stitch a quilt of their wings find a working surface
            of 20 square miles,
        To understand how many we killed that summer imagine
            the weight of 80,000 tons.
        If you can.

To make sense of war,
of insanity—
Imagine fear and power.
If you can.

Katydid

TIM MYERS

After the bug man came in a clean white truck,
casting a seasoned eye over lawn and hedges,
wielding his big spray canister, because
the wasps above the grass had become too many—
thinking themselves Subetai's Golden Horde,
black-striped amber bodies gleaming, flitting, droning—

after the bug man came,
a lime-green fellow climbed our sliding door,
with hook-and-sucker feet so deftly rising—
with more hands than we have put bits of food
into his mouth. We do that too.
I could see his green abdomen
swelling and emptying as he took in air, like a chest;
imagined a green heartbeat.
His wings mimicked leaves, his mouth had protruding parts;
but he looked around, like we do.

Lawn-dog, he made the glass climb; then fell; and then,
shimmering green against the gray porch cement,
antennae unblemished, in the flush of his adulthood
quietly folded his leaflike wings
and died.

Bug-Eyed in Love

CHRISTINE VALENTINE

It was July 1965. I was engaged and crazy in love. My fiancé, a man twenty-five years my senior, lived in a house on top of a hill above the tiny village of Birney, Montana. Appropriately called Hill House, it was built from logs by his first wife. He had been widowed four years previously.

I met him in the fall of 1964, and we courted through the winter months, becoming engaged in the spring. We often cooked supper for one another, and on this warm evening we were seated at the dining room table in his house, both enjoying a steak. The conversation flowed as we were enjoying ourselves, when suddenly his eyes got large. He sucked in his breath and the conversation ceased.

"Now don't let me alarm you," he said. "Just stay where you are, look straight ahead, and don't watch what I do. Just don't look." He got up from the table, went into the mud room, and a moment later I heard scuffling and the slam of a screen door. He eventually returned and said, "I meant to tell you about this. There are some critters that come in the house once in a while, not very often, but they look quite scary."

"Why didn't you mention this before?" I asked, thinking snakes, in particular rattlers that I had seen the previous summer. He looked perplexed and said, "I thought you might not marry me if you knew about them."

With assurance from him that it was not a snake, I told him that critters were not likely to interfere with making our love nest. He said he would save the next one that dropped in unannounced to show me.

In fact, however, one did not appear until after we were married. One day when I was cleaning, I found a horrendous-looking insect in the cold air return. The creature was about two and a half inches long, and its bulbous abdomen was glossy light brown with stripes. Its head, at least a third of its total length, was large, round, and with nasty-looking mandibles. The spiny legs had claws that somewhat resembled those of a crab.

After hearing my screams, my husband came rushing in, looked at it and said, "That's the critter I told you about last summer. They call them Baby Bugs around here." This one was dead and hastily dispatched out the back door in a dustpan.

One day a few months later while looking along the bookshelves, I came across a slim volume titled *Poisonous Dwellers of the Desert* by Natt N. Dodge.* Toward the back of the book there was a section titled "Harmless Creatures Mistakenly Believed Poisonous" with a picture of our Baby Bug.

I read that *Stenopelmatus fuscus,* known as Jerusalem Cricket, is harmless although it can bite if handled roughly. It generally lives in wood piles or under the earth. Some Native Americans refer to it as Who-tze-neh (Old Bald-Headed Man), and in Spanish it is called "Niña de la Tierra" (Child of the Earth). I suppose with our semi-arid climate in the summer months it migrates into the earth in our basement area and then into places where we can see it.

In 1972 I was widowed, and a few years later I married a man from the East Coast. We moved back to Montana to the same dwelling, and I had to initiate him into Baby Bug procedures. Nowadays we usually cover them with an ash tray, drinking glass, or other handy container, slide a catalog or thin paper object beneath, and ceremoniously dispatch them out to the woodpile where they can live in *Stenopelmatus* heaven. They no longer excite me, but we usually keep a dead one around for entertaining visitors!

---

* Natt N. Dodge, *Poisonous Dwellers of the Desert,* Southwestern Monuments Association Popular Ser. 3, ed. Dale Stuart King, 3rd ed. (Santa Fe: Southwestern Monuments Assn., 1949) 39-40.

Night Music

BOO HEISEY

She wanted night music.
It seemed odd
going to a pet store
for music.
"How much are crickets?" she asked, naively.
"Seven cents apiece."
"Give me ten."
"What size?"
"What size? I don't know. I want them for night music, what size
    do you suggest?"
"We sell them for pet food. What size do you want?"
"Give me males."
"What size?"
"It doesn't matter!"
He scooped up ten, put them in a plastic bag,
filled it with air.
She paid him 70 cents plus five cents tax,
though there shouldn't be sales tax on food.

She scattered them throughout her yard.
The ones in the front yard are silent. They never did make noise.
Either females
or food indeed
for what walks the night.

The backyard ensemble makes fine night music,
and at only 75 cents,
a bargain.

Lepidoptera

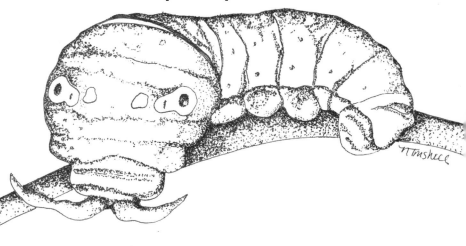

High Crimes and Caterpillars

ROBERT MICHAEL PYLE

Interstate Five, from the Columbia River to Puget Sound, passes through a pleasing array of backdrops: from the blackish green of Douglas fir fringes to the autumn scarlet curtains of vine maples south of Olympia, from the broad Nisqually Flats and the tidal apron of the Olympics on the west to the ever-improbable white giant of Rainier on the east. Of course there are also the dreary miles, more every year, of feral capitalism in rut, spilling out from the cities. Where the mercantile dreck runs together between Centralia and Chehalis, a particular billboard of strong opinion always helps to relieve the tedium. Recently, the sign revealed what the owner apparently thought was the worst thing he could say about the worst person in the world: "Saddam Hussein is a human worm."

What kind of a derogation is that? "Earthworm," if that's what was meant, names an animal highly beneficial to the soil. Charles Darwin demonstrated long ago that earthworms profoundly mold the landscape itself. However, I suspect the word "worm" on the billboard didn't refer to annelids at all, but rather to "caterpillar"—as in cutworm, tomato hornworm, maple spanworm, or cabbage worm. Fair enough. Caterpillars look rather wormlike, especially if you ignore their six true legs, four pairs of grasping prolegs, anal prolegs, outrageous colors, and various ornamentation such as horns, tubercles, and branched spines. *Sort of* wormlike. But the fact is, caterpillars are simply the larval incarnation of butterflies and moths: the second stage in Lepidoptera metamorphosis. Yet I've way too often heard people say they love butterflies but hate caterpillars, and kill them whenever they get the chance.

In fact, relatively few species of caterpillars do us harm. True enough, some kinds such as gypsy moths, spruce budworms, Douglas-fir tussock moths, certain noctuids (cutworms), leaf rollers, root borers, and minute larvae of little wheaten clothes moths can indeed become major competitors for food and fiber. But Lepidoptera is probably the fourth most diverse group of organisms, and the vast majority are beneficial or benign with respect to human needs, and dramatically important in food webs and ecosystems. Got songbirds? Then you've also got caterpillars. Want butterflies? No caterpillars, no butterflies: that's the deal. Natural systems deprived of their larvae are cruising for collapse. The mass application of DDT for gypsy moths in the 'fifties, with its unintended bird mortality, not only prompted Rachel Carson's *Silent Spring* but also rid the woods of luna moths, bats, and other wonders and vital elements for decades.

Now, when control agencies fight gypsy moths, tussock moths, or spruce budworms, they often use a bacterial larvicide called *Btk*. The organism, *Bacillus thuringiensis kurstacki*, produces a toxin lethal to lepidopterous larvae. Because it is a naturally occurring bacterium, its fans call it an "organic" alternative to pesticides, and misrepresent it as being selective. In fact, it kills all Lepidoptera equally. When sprayed on forests, *Btk* may kill upwards of ninety percent of butterfly and moth larvae in terms of both species and biomass, according to studies by Oregon State University entomologist Jeff Miller and others.

Meretricious suppliers of *Btk* advise gardeners to use it against "cabbage worms." They don't mention that doing so will spoil your garden for butterflies. (Of course, chemical pesticides will do the same.) The velvet green tubelets that make lace out of broccoli are of course caterpillars, not worms, and they will become cabbage butterflies, not moths. I believe that people routinely designate them so because they want their pests to be moths, not butterflies. But I find it no great task to pluck the larvae off the crucifers; or if they sneak in and get steamed, why, that's just a little more protein for dinner. Besides, how much cabbage can you eat? I urge living with cabbage butterflies and planting a little extra kale or sprouts, some for them, some for you; then enjoying their early, silky flight: "Two white / butterflies are doing a jig, / going higher and / higher," as poet Robert Sund described them.

Even the imposing dragonets that are tomato hornworms have their points. These finger-sized green cylinders with blue slashes on their sides and impressive horns on their butts are actually the youths of sphinx moths (*aka* hawk or hummingbird moths). When you see dusky hummingbirds hovering at the four o'clocks or petunias in the gloaming, those are sphinx moths, sucking up nectar with their long drinking-straw proboscides. One of these is famous for its existence having been predicted by Darwin, who knew there had to be a pollinator for the Madagascan orchid *Angraecum sesquipedale*, with its foot-and-a-half long nectar spur. After the moth was found, bearing a proboscis long enough for the job, it was named accordingly: now *Xanthopan morgani praedicta*. And in fact, all sphinx moths are major pollinators of night-blooming flowers, as are many other moths. A world devoid of caterpillars would be a largely sexless world for flowers, not to mention depriving plants of their major partners in the co-adaptive dance.

True, hornworms can make a mess of the tomatoes, but a related species aids public health by attacking chiefly tobacco. And I personally found them extraordinarily useful on one occasion, when I was hired to provide and wrangle caterpillars for a futuristic Tom Selleck movie involving robots. My larvae were meant to munch on corn, then be plucked by an agro-robot that subsequently ran amok, requiring policeman Selleck's attentions. The only photogenic larvae I could find that wet spring were a few dozen

Manduca sexta sphinxes that were about to be disposed of by a university laboratory. I shared an air-conditioned trailer with Selleck's stunt and camera doubles. They gravely discussed the relative merits of gold, women, and tequila, and I showed them my larvae. When our scene came, the first beast chosen performed admirably. Later I released the rest in my friend's potato patch, where they happily nibbled the leaves without harming the spuds below. The evening primroses would feel their probing ministrations the following spring.

There is nothing like the surprise of watching a tiny green sphere that appears on a dill leaf in your garden give forth a white-saddled black little wormlet, who crawls and eats and grows, molts into a bigger and bigger bird-turd mimic and then into a glorious green, yellow, and black-ringed caterpillar that will eventually disappear, only to go walkabout, pupate on a distant wall or trunk as a thorn-like brown or green chrysalis, hide away for the winter, and

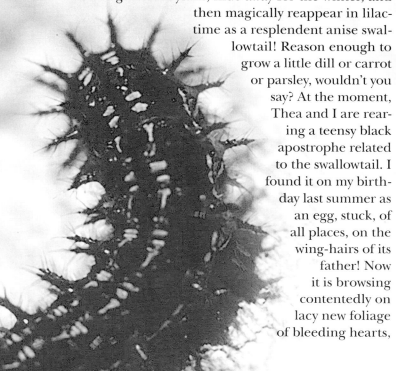

then magically reappear in lilac-time as a resplendent anise swallowtail! Reason enough to grow a little dill or carrot or parsley, wouldn't you say? At the moment, Thea and I are rearing a teensy black apostrophe related to the swallowtail. I found it on my birthday last summer as an egg, stuck, of all places, on the wing-hairs of its father! Now it is browsing contentedly on lacy new foliage of bleeding hearts, and if all goes well, it will become a big, linen-white, cherry-and-coal spotted Clodius parnassian butterfly in June—and then, against all odds, fly away.

I haven't even spoken of the exquisite patterns and thrilling beauty of many caterpillars, such as the massive emerald Polyphemus, studded with ruby and turquoise, or the vast ebony-and-lemon cigar with a little red horn we saw in El Salvador recently; of the astonishing adaptations of the candy-striped and tentacled juvenile monarch or the perfect stick-like pose of the geometrids we call inchworms; nor of Caterpillar as giver of wisdom and delight, whom Alice met in Wonderland. What I am trying to say is that far from some contemptible "worms" to be squashed at the drop of a boot, caterpillars are among the world's glories, much to be celebrated. Going organic, saving habitat, wildly abandoning prejudice as you go, you can make the world a fitter place for children and caterpillars; and then, like children, pausing to notice, watch, and touch, you can find the world's fascination all over again. As ever, tolerance is its own reward.

Time

CAROL N. KANTER

Puerile, plump,
the caterpillar pulls
the middle of its fleshy cylinder
into a lucky horseshoe loop—
a leaner on the air—
scootches forward,
makes tracks, seems
to meander

(determined though to stalk life)

scents a marigold,
  munches a spinach leaf,
    catches vistas from a high branch
      of oak or sycamore,
        sleeps amid corn silk

to wake from long, snug dreams

alone,
a dark chill
on new wet wings,
silent
slick of cambium,
cradle leaking
magic.

Moth, Magnified*

LYNNE BAMA

Is this the drab insect
that blunders on screens,
careens around bulbs,
the dimwitted, nondescript
chewer of clothes?
Now I see
what we missed.

Caped with the gorgeous brocades of a doge,
the bright feathers and fur of an Inca cacique,
crowned with a pair of silver horns,
the rainbow soul of the worm takes wing
for the fatal kingdom of night.

* This poem was inspired by digital images of moths which appeared in the May 2002 issue of *National Geographic*.

Hymenoptera

Traffic

JAY UDALL

All along the dirt path
as far as I care to look
a streaming highway
of frenetic ants connects
great cities, small towns
and wilderness between,
moved as if by some
insistent current running
through each tiny black body
venturing through the local
terrain of the infinite,
stopping, starting, going,
going—so intent, this wanting—
like that which moves
these two feet.

Why I Washed the Cloth Which Was Not Even Dirty

ELISAVIETTA RITCHIE

The tablecloth's alive with tiny ants
like three strung flecks of pepper on six legs.
The pattern's blue-and-brown batik so they
don't show till five invade my laptop. Ants
are not true bugs so I can't phone the whiz
who de-bugs our computers. I won't call
exterminators with their poison sprays.
Come winter, sometimes insects disappear.
Now spring: ants scan my poems, replace my words,
recalculate my thoughts, write their own books …

Voice of the Harvester Ant

LYNNE BAMA

There is no light here,
and we have no ears
for sound. We speak
in molecules. Our city hangs
inside the tunneled ground,
a chandelier filled up with night.

We worship her who is
the source of all, unmoving
in a perfumed basement shrine—
mother of ten thousand
armed and bearded nuns
who execute a sacred
and obscure design.

You who pass before the sun
like clouds or gods, and never
see us underneath your feet
are learning how to build;
our shadowed labyrinths have
endured for thirty million years
and will persist long after
you are obsolete.

Wasp

LOU MASSON

Green carpet did not hide
the hole beneath the casket,
nor did the drone
of the well-intended priest
fill the emptiness left
by my mother who lay forever
in the pall of the past
that fell upon the family.
Drops of dew on shoe toes
gathered like tears,
where we stood
with loss, with our fears,
barely aware of that other
drone, the buzz of the wasp
busy in the way of wasps
about the floral wreaths.
Each of us stepped back,
ducked our heads,
anxious, then relieved
when he flew off,
all now aware
that he had stung us all
with the blasphemy
of the living's present.

Apology to the Wasps

SARA LITTLECROW-RUSSELL

Today I took out some biochemical weapons and
blasted your nest like it was a third world country.
I was the United States Air Force,
and it felt good to be so powerful
until I saw all of you
trailing shredded wings
and staggering on disintegrating legs,
while you tried desperately to save the eggs
you had stung to protect.

The poison bubbled
from the crevasses around your nest
dripping down the walls.
As if searching for new life
it oozed toward a spider.

I shooed the spider from its path
and wondered at how easy it is to keep alive
my allies who eat mosquitoes and biting gnats,
as I destroy you.

The Honey Bee in America: An Organism of Contradictions

JOHN F. BARTHELL

Few animal invasions have been as spectacular as that of the Africanized honey bee in the Americas. For nearly three decades the northern front of the invasion traveled at breakneck speed (as fast as 300 miles per year) from its release point in Brazil during the 1950s to the southern United States in the early 1990s. As an undergraduate student, I cut my academic teeth while studying aspects of this invasion in Central America. The sight of undulating, airborne bee swarms crossing desolate stretches of the Pan American highway ahead of our four-wheel-drive vehicle remains an indelible memory for me. So also are memories of honey bee swarms hanging like oversized fruits among tree branches along the same route and the low, vibratory rumble of swarms passing overhead in the field. Seeing this invasion process firsthand deeply impressed me and initiated a professional odyssey that I continue today while studying invasive bee species.

With all the attention surrounding the Africanized bee, few people realize that the honey bee we have benefited from for centuries is also an introduction to the New World. True to its common name, the European bee originally took wing in the eastern United States in the early 1600s after being transported there by Europeans. Both types of bees are recognized as subspecies or geographic races of the common honey bee species, *Apis mellifera*. They can potentially interbreed (hence the term "Africanized"), but they differ markedly in certain respects. Aggression is the most storied aspect of the

Africanized bee, a trait generally assumed to be a behavioral holdover from central Africa where predators, including humans, intent on robbing nests produced in these bees a hair-trigger response to intruders.

I can recall the ferocity of Africanized bees as I—wearing a bee suit and veil, fortunately—collected samples from a nest embedded in the wall of a ranch workshop in northern Costa Rica. (A year later, in a tragic coincidence of factors, a man lost his life to honey bees on another portion of the same ranch.) But despite this well-documented aspect of Africanized honey bees, it is important to recognize that such acts of aggression take place primarily as a means of defending the nest. It may not be too far afield to try to understand this instinct by comparing our own human trepidation about the appearance of strangers around our homes—the site of our most treasured possessions and loved ones. Honey bees are rightly considered to be defensive, not offensive, organisms, but this distinction will likely remain ambiguous during this bee's cohabitation with humans in America.

Aristotle was one of the first people to write about honey bee behavior when he recounted the recruitment of female worker bees in the nest to flowers by other females that had previously foraged at the same food source. During the 1940s the German behaviorist Karl von Frisch postulated that these foragers recruit their hive-mates by conveying the location of food sources through a language. Using so-called "fan" and "step" experiments, von Frisch described how a *waggle dance* (a rapidly run figure-eight pattern) contains information on the direction and distance to flowers. This celebrated discovery found a wide audience of supporters and still occupies the efforts of behavioral ecologists across the world.

The reception of the dance language in the United States developed a mixed response. In the early 1960s, as an advocate

of the dance language, zoologist Adrian Wenner began studying how information might be transmitted during the dance
through sound production. However, as his studies progressed
and collaborations with students and colleagues expanded,
he found contradictions to the language hypothesis, including the unexpectedly long time it takes recruited bees to find
a food source. Experiments with his colleague, Patrick Wells,
demonstrated that odor, not language, was the key to understanding how honey bees locate their food. Subsequently, the
now often-cited "misdirection experiment" of James Gould
and emerging German studies on robotic bees that dance
on command support von Frisch's language hypothesis. But
the debate produced strident disagreement, even acrimony,
among the competing camps. Indeed, Wenner withdrew from
the scientific debate for a twenty-year period to gain a philosophical perspective on the episode. (He later provided his
conclusions on the controversy in a book written with his colleague Patrick Wells.) The language debate remains alive in
the scientific literature today and will require the test of time
and independent replication of the original experiments,
which is the final recourse in any scientific standoff, to fully
resolve itself.

In addition to the intrigue surrounding its social organization and communication system, the honey bee has an
enormous economic role in American agriculture. Most
people associate the bee with the honey we harvest—or perhaps, more accurately, "rob"—from its hard-earned cache
in the hive, but its largest contribution to our society comes
as a pollinator of our crops. About one-third of the food we
eat is provided to us through pollinators, with the honey
bee responsible for the majority of that amount. Honey bee
contributions to the North American agricultural economy
total several billion dollars annually, with some estimates
up to tens of billions. In California, more than forty crops
are pollinated by honey bees with one crop alone, almonds,
accounting for nearly a billion dollars in annual value. On
a per bee basis, Africanized honey bees can pollinate flow-

ers as well, some experts argue better, than European honey bees. Unfortunately, the Africanized bee's aggressive nature and tendency to leave hives unexpectedly through a behavior known as *absconding* makes these bees unreliable in an industry that requires moving hives long distances on flatbed trucks. It was this concern, among others, that moved the United States Department of Agriculture to collaborate with Mexico during the 1980s and propose a "bee barrier" (using "swarm traps" as weapons) as a way to stem the flow of Africanized swarms advancing northward to Texas. Not only did the bees reach Texas, however, but feral populations now reside throughout the southwestern United States. In combination with the inadvertent introduction of the parasitic varroa mite in the late 1980s, many fear that the Africanized bee invasion will further suppress European honey bee pollination. One estimate indicates that the number of honey bee colonies in the United States has already declined by one-fourth.

Despite their ubiquity, honey bees represent just a single species among nearly four thousand bee species in North America. Perhaps spurred by the 1996 publication of *The Forgotten Pollinators* by Stephen Buchmann and Gary Nabhan, biologists and conservationists have begun to ask anew what effects honey bees have on so many native pollinators as well as how they affect the plants they visit for nectar and pollen. A subsequent overview of this subject by the ecologist Vivian Butz Huryn, which appeared in the *Quarterly Review of Biology* in 1997, indicates that little evidence exists to indict honey bees for negatively impacting our native pollination systems.[*]

My own work with colleagues from the University of California and The Nature Conservancy indicates that honey bees promote seed production in yellow star-thistle, a noxious weed that covers significant portions of western states such as California, Oregon, Washington, and Idaho. This plant is toxic to horses, and it blankets millions of acres of valuable rangeland with its distinctive yellow and very spiny flower heads. Ironically, yellow star-thistle also appears in some of the earliest accounts of American honey plants and is recognized for the delicious, distinctively colored honey that bees produce from the plant's nectar. The many honey-producing beekeepers in the western United States may therefore view the honey bee's relationship with this "weed" quite differently from ranchers or conservationists.

How should we interpret the honey bee's role in American ecosystems? Few other species so eloquently illustrate the complexities of intentionally introduced species. Although the honey bee is inextricably and positively linked to the history of American agriculture, growing populations of the Africanized form of the bee in the western United States potentially threaten billions of dollars of bee-pollinated crops. Fiscal considerations aside, what ecological effects have we overlooked for the nearly four centuries that honey bees have occupied American ecosystems? Even long-held beliefs about the parallels between our own social characteristics (including language) and those of honey bees do not escape controversial questions.

I cannot help but feel that the honey bee reflects our own human condition as organisms on the go, virtually unrestricted in the terrestrial habitats we can inhabit on the planet. But any organism that enters a new region leaves a footprint among the patterns and processes that define that environment in its native form. In the case of the honey bee, it seems, interpreting that footprint often leads to contradictory conclusions. A pest? Surely no organism that enriches us so much economically and culturally deserves such a moniker. Perhaps, instead, the honey bee's image can best be viewed as a reflection of the paradox of our own desires to modify and yet preserve components of Nature we view as important to our humanity. The enigmatic honey bee has played a complicated and sometimes awkward role with respect to these contrasting goals, particularly in the American West.

* Vivian M. Butz Huryn, "Ecological Impacts of Introduced Honey Bees," *Quarterly Review of Biology* 72.3 (1997): 275-297.

Yellow Jacket

JOHN SULLIVAN

flies
so close

back
and forth

fans
my sweaty forearm

Diptera

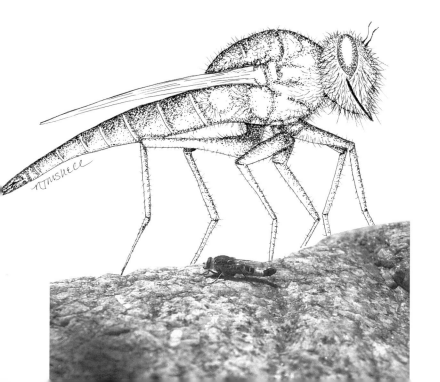

Gnats

KENNETH POBO

Some living things excel at
annoying.

Think of people who annoy you.

My neighbors keep
their German Shepherd out 24/7.
My boss fires my friends.
A snotty teller clucks when
I hand her a Canadian check.
Gnats

annoy.
When Stan and I walk in the June
woods, I do a tap dance,
slap, swat, put fingers in my ears,
rub dead gnats from my eyes. Damn

them! They surround him—
he says I walk in a "cloud"
of gnats. A high-pitched
buzz builds
till I can't take it, break

into a run back to the cabin
where I wash my hair, black bodies
dotting a white sink—

the silence a relief,
the quiet after mass murder.

A Brief Portrait of a "Useless" Insect

KEVIN M. O'NEILL

Insects are not popular animals. I suppose that most people would grant that honey bees are useful if they are some safe distance away. And perhaps butterflies are sort of appealing, though most men would not admit it. But attention tends to focus on the pests that give you malaria, eat your tomatoes, or simply land on your potato salad. In this view, the nameless hoards of harmless, but apparently useless and certainly unappealing, insects can be conveniently and deliberately ignored.

Entomologists themselves are thought to be useful insofar as they eliminate pests, and if they express an actual fascination with "useless" insects, they may be regarded as nerds or kooky eccentrics (and perhaps wasters of taxpayer dollars). I'll admit only to being an eccentric, one who has yet to convince his entomophobic friends and relatives that watching insects is more gratifying than watching TV. As a university entomologist, I have done my duty with pests (grasshoppers) and useful insects (crop pollinators), but have always set aside time for "useless" insects. In my case, that means those insects generally known as digger wasps and robber flies, both of which are common throughout the western U.S., but usually overlooked.

Of course, most insects in the West are not nameless, though their technical Latin names are often so bewildering that they might as well be. I once studied a wasp whose only specific name was *Bembecinus quinquespinosus* (not as convenient and amusing as that of the wasp *Aha ha*, but not as tortuous as that of the fly *Parastratiosphecomyia stratiosphecomyioides*). Another of my research subjects goes by the slightly more reasonable name of *Efferia staminea*, "*Efferia*" being appropriately derived from the Latin word for "fierce" or "savage." (A loose translation of its original name, *Erax stamineus* — "to love fiber"—provides no insight into its nature because it doesn't eat whole grain foods.) *Efferia staminea* is one of the robber flies, but it has no more specific "common name." The lack of a specific common name for an insect (like "monarch butterfly") is perhaps the best clue that you are working with something that not many people care about. A second clue for me was that entering *"Efferia staminea"* into an internet search engine led me, unhelpfully, to my own home page.

The jury is out on whether *Efferia staminea* is "useless" in the myopic human view. It does kill grasshoppers, but it also kills insects that eat grasshoppers, and the balance of its overall effect has yet to be determined. *Efferia staminea* are easy to ignore because they live close to the ground on grasslands, and they don't bite you, buzz around your head, or eat your garden. What attracts me to these insects is their lifestyle, one that includes sunbathing, ambushing of prey, a venomous "bite," cannibalism, playing dead, and airborne sex. Importantly, they are also big enough to be clearly observed several feet away, and they exhibit a variety of readily interpretable behaviors, in contrast to those insects that seem to aimlessly fly around in circles or sit around apparently doing nothing.

Admittedly, if you are impressed mainly by the size of an organism, an inch-long *Efferia staminea* may be a yawner. But mentally scale yourself down to the size of a robber fly, and you will see something impressive. *Efferia staminea* has a formidable look about it that suggests this is no wimpy plant-feeder. And it looks nothing like the housefly on your window-pane. On its head: large bulging eyes (for tracking down fast-moving prey) and a robust, downwardly pointing "beak" (for impaling prey). On its thorax: a large hump (containing massive flight muscles for powering its ambushes) and long bristly legs (for clutching prey). On its abdomen: silvery white hairs that glisten in the sun and, on males, an extravagant erect protuberance that covers a set of genitals that look as if they could open a beer can. To me, these insects appear more fearsome (and much more plausible) than the average creatures in science fiction films, which often look too poorly designed to survive even an hour in the wild.

As a killing machine in the context of its own world, *Efferia staminea* is a combination of hawk and leopard: a flying predator that ambushes prey as small as a midge but sometimes as large as itself. It is true that *Efferia staminea* spend a lot of time sitting, but even then they constantly shift about to carefully manipulate exposure to sunlight and regulate body temperature. From these perches, they rapidly ambush passing insects that are captured in midair, carried in flight to another perch, and injected with a venom- and enzyme-laden saliva that both paralyzes the prey and digests its innards. They then leisurely suck in the predigested soup, leaving the prey a drained, limp, and dead husk. To make matters more exciting, *Efferia staminea* are frequent cannibals, though they can usually only cannibalize robber flies smaller than themselves. Small *Efferia staminea* can only prey on smaller species of robber flies, but large *Efferia staminea* can be victimized by larger species. It's a fly-eat-fly world out there! However, they often avoid attacks by fellow robber flies by falling to the ground and playing dead. When males and females are not eating each other, they may engage in a brief noisy courtship, coupling in midair and copulating while hanging from a plant. Does this all sound fun to watch, or is it just me?

Hundreds of hours watching *Efferia staminea* has not made me a better softball player, more interesting at parties, or more attractive to women, and it has certainly not gained me the admiration of the bug-snubbers of the world. But I am not afraid to admit that I find the fierce, functional looks of *Efferia staminea* aesthetically pleasing and its behavior captivating, and I am convinced that entomophobes are missing something. My advice: turn off the TV, scale down your world, and spend some time looking at "useless" insects. You might find your inner entomophile, and it's commercial-free viewing too.

Epiphany

DIANALEE VELIE

The fly circled the lipsticked
rim of her Pepsi can,
landing in jubilant victory.
Twice I watched her drink.
Twice I watched the fly disembark,
circle, and spitefully, or religiously,
land on the rim of her can
in the exact spot her lips kept touching.

I pictured little fly feet
coated with the red
warning of her lipstick
and the danger of *E. coli*,
Egyptian encephalitis,
and other deadly, insect borne
afflictions. Continually shooing
the fly away, she laughed.

In that epiphany,
I recognized I had forgotten how.

Coleoptera

Territorial Dispute

JANE MAYES

Black beetle with flimsy antennae,
        you land on my clipboard. Surprised,
you shyly crawl to the underside
        seeking safety and anonymity;
but I turn it over and expose you again.
Reflexively I flick you away,
        without knowing why.

We study each other where you land.
Who will flinch first?
Curiosity draws me nearer
        to count your legs, and
finding only five, I am filled with guilt
        until I see you crawl away
        quite adroitly. But now you circle 'round
and crawl up the back leg of my chair.

Are you bent on revenge,
        or merely reclaiming your home
that I mistakenly thought was my chair?

The Colorado Potato Beetle

FRED BROSSY

This is a story of an extraordinary journey of a widely eaten, basic vegetable: the potato, and a destructive "pest" that farmers love to hate and yet one that this farmer has come to respect: the Colorado potato beetle. *Leptinotarsa decemlineata* is a leaf-eating beetle of the insect family Chrysomelidae, which at both its larval and adult stages feeds on the leaves of potatoes and other plants of the night-shade family (Solanaceae). It can cause significant damage to potato crops, reducing yields substantially. However, as the potato beetle is not a native of South America where the potato (*Solanum tuberosum*) originated, it is not even a "pest" in the potato's original habitat. In fact, if it were not for the ever-increasing worldwide popularity of the potato since it was "discovered" by the Spanish explorers in Peru almost five hundred years ago—and the relatively recent, growing global appetite for french fries, the potato beetle would likely not even be considered a pest at all. Moreover, due to this beetle's considerable adaptability, if one looks beyond the potential economic damage of which it is capable, the potato beetle is quite a remarkable insect. It has thus far adapted to climatic conditions worldwide and quite unlike those of its original habitat, as well as succeeded in developing resistance to virtually every pesticide used to control it.

The association between the beetle and the potato plant is a result of two very interesting migrations. For starters, the beetle did not originate in Colorado, but is native to Mexico where it evolved with burweed (*Solanum rostratum*), a commonly occurring plant of the Solanaceae family. As its name suggests, this plant forms a bur around its seedpod, which, according to Wenhua Lu and James Lazell in "The Voyage of the Beetle," an article that appeared in *Natural History* in 1996, facilitated its movement from Mexico to Texas by allowing the seedpod to cling to the coats of longhorn cattle that had been introduced to that country by the Spanish.* In turn, after this plant became established in Texas, it continued to migrate farther north by attaching to the woolly fur of bison, hence its common name, buffalo burweed. Of course, the beetle followed the plant north as well. In 1819, naturalist Thomas Say noted the beetle on the Great Plains while he was camped on the Missouri River near the present border of Nebraska and Iowa.

Several hundred years previously, in the late 1500s, the Spanish had introduced the potato to Europe, although it did not arrive in North America until about 1719. The Americans brought the potato with them as they settled the West, and apparently the beetle and the potato first encountered each other in Nebraska around 1859. It is thought that the subspecies of the beetle which has since become a serious "pest" in most potato-growing regions was actually a genetic mutation of the original species. At any rate, as the potato plant did not co-evolve with the beetle, it was not resistant to the defoliation caused by the insect. The beetle apparently found potato plants quite tasty and chewed its way east, devastating potato fields the whole way. Within a decade, it had reached the East Coast, becoming a considerable problem in New England, and actually crossed the Atlantic to Britain shortly thereafter. It was, however, eventually eradicated from England, and is no longer a "pest" there, although it occurs throughout Europe.

As suggested previously, the potato beetle's ability to adapt is quite impressive. Not only did this insect successfully acquire a completely new host plant within a very short period of time, but it also managed to live and thrive in climates quite different from its native neo-tropical habitat. That an insect which originated in a warm environment such as central Mexico could survive the subfreezing winters of the northern United States and Europe is truly amazing. Because members of Solanaceae, its host-plant family, contain poisonous alkaloids, the beetle is accustomed to a diet of toxins and, beginning with its resistance to DDT, has proved hard to control for any length of time with pesticides. Like many specific insect crop "pests" today, which only cause problems for a particular host crop that the insects prefer, the potato beetle is really only a "pest" for farmers who grow potatoes, such as myself. Due to the overpopulation of one plant species that is common to modern monocrop agroecosystems, most of the time the insect "pests" are merely fulfilling the ecological role of attempting to balance the crop environment by reducing the overpopulation. Thus from my perspective as an organic farmer trying to apply agroecological principles to my farm, if a crop is no longer planted as a monoculture, but instead is interplanted with other crops within a given field (thereby adding diversity to the agroecosystem), many crop "pests" are theoretically no longer as great a problem. However, because of the scale at which we grow potatoes, and the logistics involved with modern harvest equipment, it is not practical to plant them as part of polycultures. Therefore, in areas where large acreages of potatoes are grown, the potato beetle will probably always be a "pest."

Although potato plants themselves have not developed resistance to potato beetles, the beetles do have natural insect enemies such as predacious ground beetles (Carabidae), which feed on the eggs, the two-spotted stinkbug (*Perillus bioculatus*), which feeds on potato beetle larvae, and even the common ladybug (*Hippodamia* spp.). Unfortunately, these natural enemies rarely occur in sufficient numbers to effectively control the potato beetles in monocrop situations. I have found that crop rotation, providing there is enough distance between potato fields from year to year, is one method to outwit this persistent insect. However, as they can reproduce on other host plants of the nightshade family, if these plants are present in the agroecosystem, as they are on our farm, the beetles will never disappear altogether. For this reason, probably the most effective way to grow potatoes in harmony with them is never to let potato beetle numbers get too large.

As I have already noted, the Colorado potato beetle is only a "pest" of those solanaceaous plants that we humans value as food, primarily potatoes, and occasionally tomatoes (*Lycopersicon esculetum*), peppers (*Capsicum annuum*), and eggplant (*Solanum melongena*). It actually plays an important role in keeping so-called "weeds" of the nightshade variety in relative balance with other plants. In fact, in dry bean (*Phaseolus vulgaris*) crops where, due to its berries that can clog harvest equipment and stain the beans, the weed hairy nightshade (*Solanum sarrachoides*) can be a considerable problem, a large potato beetle population is an asset, keeping the nightshade plants eaten back to the point that they do not flower and set seed. Consequently, even though the potato beetle can be a nightmare for my potato crops, as an organic farmer, I welcome them in my bean fields.

So, the inclusion of the Colorado potato beetle in the "pest" category depends entirely on one's perspective. If you are a gardener, more than likely the scale at which you grow potatoes is such that picking the beetles off the plants by hand can control the damage they cause. At the farm scale, however, potato beetles are potentially a very serious "pest," especially if a large acreage of potatoes is being grown. On the other hand, in regard to other crops, not only are these beetles not at all "pests," but they can even be allies. From a biological perspective, and as a farmer continually striving to farm in harmony with the natural world, it is hard not to respect and admire the adaptability of *Leptinotarsa decemlineata*.

* Wenhua Lu and James Lazell, "The Voyage of the Beetle," *Natural History* Jan. 1996: 37-39.

Of Other Orders

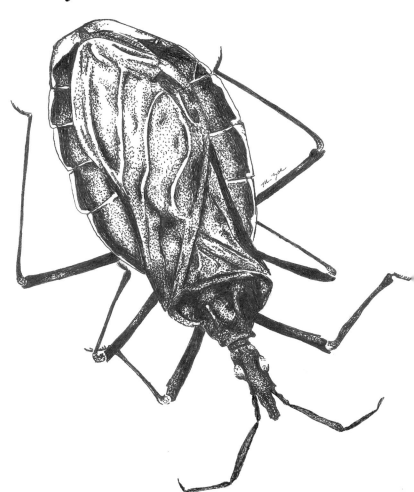

Never Kiss
a Walapai Tiger

HARLEY G. SHAW

I was sleeping deeply, lusciously, without dreams. The kind of sleep we all wish for when we retire each night. Suddenly the bedroom light came on and the quilt was jerked violently from my body. My heart was instantly pounding, even before I was fully awake. Was this the KGB, the CIA, or the FBI bursting into my room so rudely? What could possibly bring about such an intrusion in the wee hours?

In truth, by the time I was half awake, I knew who had perpetrated the attack. And I knew the culprit being pursued wasn't me. The "agent" worked for no government enforcement bureau. In fact, seconds earlier, she had been snuggled alongside of me, deep in her own slumber. Yes, the person who had mounted such a violent attack was my wife, Patty. The villain she pursued was a creature, plain and simple, that was less than one inch in length and looked something like the harmless "squash bug" that lives in most folks' gardens.

But this bug was not quite so harmless, and at least one of its local names, Walapai tiger, betrayed its true nature. I had heard of this secretive insect during most of my youth, usually under the name of kissing bug. This name apparently derives from the fact that it often bites people when they are covered up in bed, hence many bites occur on the face. The lips appear to be particularly tasty. I would say that it is a long reach, however, to call its bite a kiss.

Later, when I took an entomology course in college, I heard the insect called a cone-nosed bug. Some people call it a cone-nosed beetle, but beetle it is not. It belongs to the order of true bugs and is classified more narrowly within the group called assassin bugs. Insofar as humans are concerned, it may be the only member of this group that earns its name. Only after Patty and I met did I develop the habit of calling it a Walapai tiger. That was its most common name around Oracle, Arizona, where Patty had spent her teen years. Even though I had spent much of my life camped out in desert habitats where this insect lives, my experience with it was nil. Outside of the entomology class collections, I had never knowingly seen one. I had never, as far as I knew, experienced its "bite," which is actually a swollen and elongated bump that raises around the point where the creature inserts its proboscis to suck the blood of its selected prey. Said prey can be most any mammal including packrats, raccoons, dogs, and humans.

Once Patty and I camped in the desert, and Walapai tigers regularly visited our camp, usually with the goal of joining us in bed. Patty, not given to such a *menage a trois*, had an uncanny ability to sense their presence and always reacted instantly. She said she could smell them. I'm convinced she did. I'm also convinced that she could have a light shining and covers ripped from the bed before she bothered to become awake. She was infallible. When she irrupted in such a manner at midnight, we always had a "Wally" in the folds of our sheet or under a pillow.

Such violent late-night behavior was not irrational. Patty has ample reason to dislike "Wallies" inhabiting our bed. Any time she fails to detect one quickly enough, it sinks its proboscis into her and leaves a stinging, itching bump that lasts for days. Fortunately, Patty seldom reacts more strongly, but her mother once had a reaction that provided ample reason to fear the Wally's kiss. She went into shock and passed out. Her blood pressure dropped to near zero. A dose of Benedryl counteracted the symptoms long enough to get her under medical care. Even so, she suffered for months from a variety of physiological responses to the bite.

The University of Arizona Agricultural Extension Service provides the following description of our southwestern species of Wally:

Adults are ½ to 1 inch long, brownish black, broad, flat but stout bodied, with 6 reddish-orange spots on each side of the abdomen, above and below. It has an elongated, cone-shaped head. The beak is slender and tapered and almost bare. It is folded back under the chest when not in use. Its wings are normally folded across the back while resting or crawling.

Wallies require a blood meal in order to lay eggs. They "nest" in dens of warm-blooded mammals, such as packrats and raccoons. They can fly and are attracted to light when searching for a victim. One of the best ways to attract Wallies is to read in bed during warm months. Their flattened body allows them to squeeze through small openings; therefore, only the tightest of houses will keep them out. They often hole up in debris, hence can inadvertently be carried inside with firewood.

When I was growing up, I heard a lot about "kissing bugs" being carriers of encephalitis. I find nothing about such a thing in the literature now, but the Latin-American version of the Wally carries an equally dreaded malady known as Chagas disease. Named after the man that described it, this disease is introduced into the bloodstream of a Wally's victim as a result of the insect's habit of defecating near the site of the bite. Irritation caused by the bite brings the victim to scratch the site, thereby rubbing the fecal material into the wound or transmitting it to the eyes or mouth. Chagas is considered to be one of the most serious human diseases in the American tropics and subtropics. Its initial symptoms are high fever, edema, and nervous disorders. If the victim survives the first attack, the disease enters a chronic phase, which may last 10-20 years. The trypanosome disease organism invades and destroys cardiac, integumentary, and nervous tissue. Victims may ultimately die due to cardiac failure resulting from such damage. Some historians have speculated that Charles Darwin contracted Chagas disease when he intentionally allowed a cone-nosed bug to bite him during his Beagle voyage. His symptoms in later life apparently fit within those described for Chagas. This disease apparently does not occur in Arizona, but it has been documented in Texas.

As I said, insofar as I know, I've never been bitten by a Wally. This makes me suspect that some people just don't smell or taste good to them.

From a purely anthropocentric viewpoint, it's not easy to find anything nice to say about Wallies. If we could shed our anthropocentricity, we might say that Wallies have value in that they give us value. That is, we are useful because we provide an occasional meal for another species. I won't try to sell that argument at the local Chamber of Commerce.

There are a few things you can do to avoid being bitten by Wallies. First, don't build a house in good woodrat habitat. Wallies may be happy to have you in the neighborhood, but many other wild creatures would just as soon have their habitat left intact. Second, keep a bright light shining away from your home during the warm months and minimize night lighting in your house. Avoid reading in bed. Finally, keep a close watch on bedding used by pets. Wallies are known for spending their days under dog beds, for instance, and then traveling the short distance to the sleeping dog at night for a meal. If humans are sleeping nearby, Wallies may seek an occasional diversified diet.

An entomologist friend searched hard for kind words about Wallies, but after considerable thought, could only be positive about the fact that they all eventually die. Obviously, one could make a case for their ecological role in preventing overpopulation of woodrats and, perhaps, other wild mammals. As an ecologist, I buy such arguments in principle, and feel that Wallies should be left alone in their native wilds. Unfortunately, we humans keep redefining the boundaries of the wilds as we build our homes more and more in the habitats of woodrats, hence Wallies and other predacious creatures. A truly positive role for Wallies would be to dissuade humans from contributing to urban sprawl. If you don't want Wallies, stay in town. Maybe the best thing about Wallies is that they help to keep humans humble. Based on this argument, we should wish for a boom in Wally populations.

American Cockroach

PHILIP MILLER

Bewhiskered,
Swift,
Whispering
On six thin legs
Across the floor
Up the wall:
Look above your head,
One stands on the ceiling,
Whiskers working
Close to the chandelier
So its body
Gleams
Before it disappears
Into a crack that seems to open
Automatically as it returns
To its snug nest
One might call
Roach Run.
If you see one of them,
Think of all the rest,
Living in closest quarters,
Touching antennae
To say hello or goodbye,
Scurrying in and out,
Each one of them
The same size
With eyes like periods,
Each one
With its own
Shade of night.

Of Lice and Kin:
A Lousy Tale

KELLY A. COFFMAN

Head lice. Some people call them *Pediculus humanus capitis*, others call them cooties. The topic alone is nearly taboo in our fear-based western culture, despite the reality that, unlike body lice (*Pediculus humanus humanus*), head lice usually pose no serious health threats to most folks, other than itchiness and the occasional secondary infection or swollen gland. Yet here in the United States, we attach the infestation of these tiny creatures with an austere and inaccurate stigma of filthiness, leaving overrun individuals feeling embarrassed and very alone.

So what if I were to label head lice as potentially fascinating teachers? Or tell you that head lice may actually have several humbling life lessons—"lice lessons"—and even a significant benefit to offer the open-minded (and willing-headed), infested human?

No, I am not proposing a national "Save the head lice" campaign, nor am I encouraging those who have never been infested to actively seek out the experience. And I surely do not mock our psychological discomfort with head lice, for I recognize the proposed evolutionary benefits to humankind's biophobias. Body lice, the close cousins of head lice, have been known to carry typhus and have caused the deaths of millions of humans.

I also know firsthand that nothing can conceal the fact that head lice are nocturnal, parasitic creatures whose entire 30-day life cycle depends upon piercing our scalps with their little siphons and feeding off *our* blood for 35 to

45 minutes at a time, several times a day. (For if they go any longer than one to two days without the help of us humans, they will dehydrate and die.) And I do not deny that the anticoagulant in the saliva they injected into my own scalp left me tossing, turning, and itching to such extremes that I sometimes felt on the verge of madness.

In face of these facts, though, I do believe that in stepping back to approach the issue with knowledge and lightheartedness, it is possible to gain a sense of respect for our sesame-sized brethren. As a recently infested person myself, I am living proof that a former lice casualty can move beyond her individual itchiness, and even beyond her society's fears, to find a space where she is able to honor the close and brief relationship she once had with head lice.

My story is nothing out of the ordinary as far as head lice tales go. At age twenty-one, I had my first encounter with serving as hostess to a real live head lice village that was founded right in the depths of my long, brown hair. Prime property was claimed behind my ears and on the nape of my neck for ideal weather conditions—warmest spots this side of the scalp. (I feel I am qualified to classify my head as an ex-village because I certainly had as many or more residents as the "average" infested person, which is less than one dozen active lice living among hundreds of dead, hatched, or living eggs.) While typically young children are more prone to infestation than adults in the United States, I guess they, being enterprising and not nit-picking creatures, made an exception for me. Apparently I served as quite the home for these critters, as I found that, according to my newly acquired knowledge of the head louse life cycle, they had been living the good life in my scalp for at least two or three months without my knowing.

Yet I must give them credit for their effective camouflage techniques, for adults are able to match their coloring to that of their human host's hair (exempting, of course, more modern tinges such as neon pink or blue). During this time of inconspicuousness—and two to three months is not an uncommon time frame for them to go undetected—the adult female louse seizes her opportunity; she is thought to lay four to ten eggs a day, mostly at night, cementing them as closely as possible to the scalp for warmth. (Ironically, careless self-cementing causes one of the most common deaths head lice experience, aside from inbreeding or rupturing due to an overindulgence at dinner time. But do not worry too much over their fragility, for no parasitic insects bother head lice themselves, and they have few real enemies aside from the mental capacities of their human hosts.)

My initial response to their surprise visit was neither one of shock nor shame. What I actually experienced was curiosity and guilt. For at the time when I identified the source of my itchiness, I was on vacation and staying with friends and family for the winter holiday season—which meant that I'd potentially brought more into their homes than hugs and Christmas cheer. Of course I noticed the first louse while staying at the home of my partner's family, and after its identity was positively confirmed by a nurse friend, the house broke into a commotion that did not stop until the day my lousy head left to fly back home. Oh, what a wonderful way to make a favorable impression on likely in-laws.

However, it was my own mother, I felt, who was without a doubt the biggest "victim" of the whole experience. She really fears the critters, no doubt because she provides child care right in her home. When I initially told her about my lice discovery, her immediate reaction led me to infer that perhaps I had acquired the infestation due to a lapse in personal hygiene. Unfortunately, I took this possibility to heart until I later learned that lice do not distinguish between clean and dirty manes, nor do they discriminate based on race or socioeconomic class. Nevertheless, my mom seemed both truly embarrassed by my infestation and also frustrated with the unexpected laundry burdens my lice and I had caused her. I must confess, though, that I was able to shed my guilt at one point; while comparing over-the-counter pediculicide treatments at the drugstore, my mom told me she wished there were a self check-out available so that no one outside the family would find out about our secret.

I feel obligated to add here that my decision to use a pediculicide treatment was a hasty one, and initially I falsely assumed that harsh, quick-fix shampoos and rinses were the best and only way to go—unless I elected for the extreme remedy of shaving my head entirely. (I decided against it, though I jealously watched as my partner, who acquired quite the infestation himself, readily shaved his lice ordeal away.)

Not too long after applying the treatments, I came to find that many experts agree that the greatest harm of head lice today is actually in the accidental misuse of the neurotoxic substances intended to eliminate lice. I would not choose the pediculicide route again and feel that the safest and surest way to get rid of head lice is to invest in a good fine-toothed comb and to make a commitment of an hour or more of intense combing until all lice and nits are gone. Ultimately I ended up calling upon this simple, laborious combing method myself when, after two pricey pediculicide treatments, the persistent little buggers were still successfully squatting up there. In addition, I read some recent studies that show head lice are increasing their resistance to pediculicide treatments.

Perhaps we could learn a thing or two from both the individual louse's determination to survive as well as the overall evolutionary tenaciousness and efficiency of the species. Take, for example, their speed. While head lice do not have wings, cannot jump, and move awkwardly on smooth surfaces, they are undoubtedly quick for their size of two to four millimeters long and can crawl across tresses at a foot per minute. This is thanks to their six hook-like claws that are each attached to the louse's version of an insect "thumb," which makes for ideal pinching from hair-vine to hair-vine in a seemingly effortless traverse through the hair jungle.

For me, all the demanding combing paid off in unexpected ways. I will never forget how this process led me to experience a genuine, primitive form of human bonding with others during several of our nit-picking sessions. I am grateful for those who provided kind grooming assistance, which reminds me of the strong influence that primate grooming efforts play on their social structures and hierarchies, and I cannot deny the strong obligation I still feel to repay those who helped groom me in my time of need. My partner's mother spent over two hours toiling above my head in the tiring rhythm of dividing, combing, spinning, and pinning my long hair up into one-by-one inch sections. Then, upon returning home, my next-door neighbor whisked me over to the family beauty shop and gave me the royal treatment, complete with a relaxing tea-tree oil shampooing, a folk remedy that her family prefers. Other alternative treatments include scalp-coating with olive oil, Vaseline, or even mayonnaise.

It seems to me that this time-consuming, manual removal invites both the groomer and "groomee" to slow down to an almost meditative state. How naturally an intimate act like voluntary nit-picking makes for provocative conversation! We marveled over the downright hardiness of those hard-to-squish bugs, toyed with ideas for lice-removal games and their point values, gossiped, and conversed about politics, men, child rearing, and other absorbing womenfolk issues. Each time I sat down for a nit-picking, it felt as if I were commencing a ritual, and I actually came to welcome it. This is no surprise, considering evolutionary psychologist Robin Dunbar's theory which proposes that language itself evolved because it served as a more efficient primate networking system than the time-consuming efforts of mutual grooming away of dirt, fleas, and lice.* I also learned that this rigorous but beneficial comb-only procedure is truly time-tested, as anthropologists have uncovered combs from early Egyptian times that are nearly identical in style to those used today. In fact, professional nit pickers who charge up to $50 an hour in major U.S. cities use the same combing tool and likely the same method as the ancients.

It has been a long time now since I've spotted any louse

neighbors frolicking about in my once booming village. I do not exactly miss them like one misses old friends. Nor can I easily forget all that crazed, midnight scratching or the feeling I got when my family shied away from giving me goodbye hugs when I was leaving at the end of my winter break. The lice and I definitely had our moment in time, just as many of our ancestors—theirs and mine—have shared over the eons. Now my head is just another lice ghost town, void of any of these itsy bitsy teacher-creatures who once captivated me with their fascinating evolutionary legacy and simple, daily existence lived out in my very own head. And now the same comb that once nitpicked its way through the formation of heart-to-heart bonding is just gathering dust in the back of my medicine cabinet. Who knows, though—I work in a kindergarten, where my fondness for children is, on occasion, matched by the interests of their other tinier "admirers." So perhaps Lady Louse and I are destined to meet again someday.

---

* Robin Dunbar, *Grooming, Gossip, and the Evolution of Language* (Cambridge: Harvard U P, 1996).

Apache Cicada: Prince of Darkness, Monarch of Light

ALLEN M. YOUNG

You fell from a branch as a tiny baby, almost ant-like, perhaps a few years ago, and burrowed into the dry, hardened earth of this windswept plain.

You, and the countless generations before, have been doing this many eons in time before the first human footprint appeared on this continent.

This is your grace, your heritage, the ecological elegance you, and myriads of other insects embossed upon this raw landscape, giving birth, over time, of intricate webs of life that help sustain us all.

Oh, but what about the footprint of humans upon your home, Apache cicada?

No doubt you survived the arrival of native peoples who did little to change the land.

But in no small measure your fate was sealed when settlers descended upon your ancient home. The land was forever changed, and not necessarily good for you, my Apache friend.

Who among us mortals today could have known the delicate state of your subterraneous abode? The earth is your home before you take to the sky and sunshine as a winged adult. You need the darkness of the earth where you plough endlessly in search of sap-filled roots—your sustenance.

Without living plants, you are doomed, little cicada. You cannot live without draining away harmlessly, drop by drop, sap from a root here, a root there, as you tunnel through the darkness. And isn't this true for millions of other insects that dine on plants?

Cicadas such as the Apache are in a pathetic state nowadays— much of their natural habitats paved over with concrete and asphalt. We are a land of shopping malls and super highways—the antithesis of what is nature.

I hope it is not goodbye to the cicadas of this continent, but a sense of dirge of impending doom and extinction in the shrill buzz of Apache cicadas calling for their mates across this blustery terrain.

So, baby cicada, born of an egg placed carefully in a branch crevice by a doting mother, your chances grow slimmer and slimmer each year as civilization claims more and more of your birthright turf to becoming a shimmering monarch buzzing away in the heat of the day, broken free from your earthen midnight existence.

And what a tragedy, for in your very being blooms your essence to the rest of the world: a symbolic bridge between the fruits of the earth, the precious nature of the landscape, and the brightness of the sun.

And Their Kin
– In No Particular
Order

Mite

KIRBY CONGDON

A pin-point, pointless,
tinier than a dot,
explores the *terra firma*
of this cold bathroom's
hard, tiled floor
—that astral desert's
enormous expanse,
dry, rootless, clean,
with no life support.
I, speechless, am mute
with no hope, help nor prayer.
A man can only gape,
head bowed,
toward another creature's life
still surviving down there.
Yet, ever rude,
I, human,
relentless,
stare!

Millipede

MELISSA BOROWICZ BETRUS

You move along in coordinated currents,
each leg a muscled eyelash sweeping the earth
striding across the inches as though it weren't
an effort or a curse bestowed by birth.
Your body, small and simple, flares its hem.
An elongated Vegas showgirl ruffling your skirt,
you draw the curious closer to the gem
that hides beneath your camouflage of dirt.
But human eyes so many times your size
can't always see the beauty in detail
or examine what your simple life implies.
We'll just be shocked to learn the world is frail.
But we'll continue at our faster pace
slowly invading even your little space.

A Saga of Sow Bugs

CB FOLLETT

Sow bugs like our hot tub,
seek a moist haven under the lip of the cover.
They live there, birth there,
one large and many tiny generations.

By day they huddle,
at night they scramble out
and eat the potted pansies on the bench.

I don't want to share those yellow faces
with sow bugs. Their appreciation
is entirely gastronomic.

Each morning I step into the hot tub
and sink down. I lift the plastic combing.
Sow bugs.
Sudden exposure confuses them,
their minds go faster than their legs,
swimming lifeguard-legs to move them
to safety.

I blow a gust of human wind and most of them
sail beyond the deck. Occasionally one falls
backward into hot water, sinks quickly.
I catch and lift it out
unfazed, legs still churning. I fling them
over the side into a one-story free-fall.

I do not need their deaths,
only relocation.
What are they thinking as they fall?
Is it like a pilot:
grandeur with a bit of the usual?

It Came from Inner Space

PATRICIA M. WOODRUFF

When my family moved from northern Nevada to Oracle, Arizona, in October 1956, our new state was in a "state of siege" by an extreme drought; water was being trucked in to the local households. Climatic history has shown us that this drought was as severe as the 1890 drought in the Southwest. Within a month of our move in October, the skies opened up. In retrospect, this was an El Nino cycle; usually the summer monsoons are absent the next summer. However, the summers of 1957 and 1958 produced wonderful, classic monsoons, and we experienced an *explosion* of critters. Every day provided a new discovery: tarantulas bigger than your hand, scorpions in every corner, "Walapai tigers" lurking and looking for blood at night, huge sun scorpions with monstrous jaws that glistened as they darted about at the speed of light. Enormous bugs and beetles, sounding like B-52 bombers, flew bumbling and crashing into circles of patio lights, and enormous Colorado River toads lumbered out of the dark to snap them up. We had rattlers, racers, king snakes, ring-necked snakes, Sonoran whipsnakes, bull snakes, Gila monsters, flies whose maggots ate live flesh, orange-legged centipedes over a foot long. We marveled at what the earth could produce, and we dutifully identified everything. However, one creature in the books eluded us—the oddly named Vinegaroon.* I often wondered what *they* were.

Almost a half century later, my husband and I moved to Hillsboro, New Mexico, a tiny town on the cusp of the Chihuahuan desert and grassland. Within a month, thunderstorms arrived. One humid evening we were surprised by a creature moving in the shadows—slow and oblivious of us. I was utterly unprepared for this six-inch critter. It appeared to be made out of miniature parts from a scrap metal pile. It was a dull rusty color; it moved deliberately, like a small machine on improbably long legs, and it smelled—like vinegar. A Vinegaroon! Its head (prosoma) appeared to be a lobster, its abdomen a flattened muffler complete with indentations, slightly bent upward as though carelessly flung into a junk heap; its arm-like pedipalps, when held "engarde," were pieces of a chainsaw chain with an inside hook at each joint. A small knurled knob on its rear abdomen supported a three-inch, thin, stiff tail (a telson) with tiny hair-like spikes (setae), which, when viewed under a hand lens, looked very much like barbed wire. It moved along on six long, jointed legs, and had *another* pair in front, at least twice as long as the others.

This rather large arachnid is related to spiders and scorpions—all eight-legged critters—but is in a family all its own.

I couldn't take my eyes off it. With its long front legs delicately tapping and waving, its pedipalps curled into two large knobs at either side of its head, it moved deliberately across the patio to the edge of the house. We placed a large active, predatory beetle in front of it. Those long front legs confused and confined the beetle. The beetle turned away from the tapping legs toward the vinegaroon's head. In a flash the chainsaw grabbers unfurled and the beetle was imprisoned!

Vinegaroons forage in corners, in leaf refuse, in dark, damp protected areas, the same space used by other arachnids, skunks, and oftentimes, larger animals. It goes about its business, quietly searching for food at dusk or calmly waiting on a wall near a light source after dark. Vinegaroons, when disturbed, have a stance that is both comically fearsome and highly effective. The tail seems to be the trigger for releasing the vinegar odor. I experimented with this idea by crawling around a vinegaroon, pretending to be a predator, smelling it and blowing on the upright tail. The creature took an immediate aggressive stance, vibrating its tail and emitting the highly acidic vinegar odor from its rear. Even a skunk would be taken aback.

Most of a vinegaroon's life is spent underground, hiding in a humid, sandy substrate. The sand holds the moisture needed for breeding, laying eggs, and especially, molting. A vinegaroon goes through four annual instars, or molts. In order to protect itself during molting, it makes a space in the sand into a protective shelter where its chitinous outer layer can harden during this period of extreme vulnerability.

We had constant visitations from vinegaroons who came in and around our old adobe home. The house had been remodeled, and the new floor had a deep layer of sand upon which brick floors were laid. The house sat on an old meander of Percha Creek, making the perfect habitat—with sand, moisture, and protection—for our new friends. Alas, for the vinegaroons that came *into* our home, the house had been sprayed with pesticides by the previous owner. We often found vinegaroons barely moving or dead in a corner. I couldn't bear to dispose of them, so I packed them gently in cotton and sent them to grandchildren or decorated various posts on our front porch with their brittle, rusty bodies.

Our new Hillsboro neighbors were horrified. "You didn't kill them? They are harmless—and they hunt cockroaches!" As I explained how they had died, I realized we had found the right place to live. We now try to remove all vinegaroons from the house as soon as we find them, hoping they survive the exposure to pesticides long ago applied.

One neighbor, upon seeing our little decorations, shared this story with us. After moving here, she awoke one morning to a slight tickling, like a nerve twitching on her legs. Upon lifting the bedcovers, she discovered a large vinegaroon using her as a hunting post. She laughed, saying that she levitated off the bed. She gathered her wits, grabbed a dustpan, and moved it outside—happy to send it on its way. She said that if this had happened when she visited, she would never have moved here, but that now "I've really grown to love them."

We have learned in many ways from vinegaroons and our other new Hillsboro friends, "We are all neighbors."

* Giant Whipscorpion, *Mastigoproctus giganteus*

Black Widow Morning

PAT ANDRUS

Were you on the *inside* or the *outside* of my screen door
when I first saw you before breakfast?
This detail is significant considering your reputation
on my list of spiders to escape.

But graceful. When I tried to coax you to crawl
onto my leaf, your fragile legs alternately touched
and sensed that leaf,
before backing away from my invitation.

And perseverance. I gently tossed your body, attached now
to a twig (your obvious transportation of choice),
at least four times down the embankment; and after every toss
but my last, you still started back up, sure no doubt
shade was available on our upper pinnacle.

Would I have treated you less kindly, if I had known
your identity?

I know there's a wolf spider living under my sink. I thought
of cleaning the whole area out a few weeks ago,
but didn't feel adventuresome opening my cupboard door
to a webbed world. And glad I didn't destroy
that sticky silk bed, as it kept a good lid on
cockroaches and stink bugs populating my rooms.

Were you *IN* my home, Black Widow? I haven't slept well
the last few nights, yet thrill at stars all bunched in black sky,
the moon setting with its shine brightening my face,
and the darkness after.
Have you also kept me awake, my subconscious
alert to your presence?

I leave you on the hillside,
unless of course you crawl back up and again
get to my screen door, or closer.

Oh my *Latrodectus hesperus,*
arachnid of my nights,
my red-hourglass-bellied female,
please depart!

Again

JAY UDALL

A speck traverses the curve
of a circular white world—
the tiniest spider I've ever seen
crawling inside yesterday's coffee cup.
I turn the cup over, rap the side
against my open palm to help him out—
too hard. Too hard. I've killed
again.

Spider Elegy

JEFF PONIEWAZ

Spider descending from ceiling
in front of my bookcase
I catch in old peanut jar I keep
to capture spiders inside
and liberate outside.
When it's halfway into the
jar I lift upward under it,
I snap on the lid and notice
toward the bottom of the jar
a spider shriveled on a shred of web.
What day did I catch you,
spider I captured to liberate
but forgot about,
detoured by some distraction
from liberating promptly?
Zen lesson: don't leave your spider
in capture jar long enough to spin
a pathetic futile starvation web.

One Morning I Was Rescued by a Worm

SARA LITTLECROW-RUSSELL

Wrapped in pinstripes and tailored wool
Like CEO's birthday present,
I join the people rushing to the train
And suddenly stumble over a man
Who has stopped to buy a *Wall Street Journal.*
We exchange smiles, stammered apologies.
I like the unruly bit of hair
That falls across his forehead.
He likes my suit.

Our smiles widen
But the 7:28 train is always on time
So I sling my law books over my shoulder
And scurry on, eyes cast down
A good commuter again.

A small worm writhes in front of me
Shriveling against the cold, dry cement.
I want to hurry on
Because I have important things to do
But then I stumble again.

Turning back, I pick up the worm
And cradle it in my hand.
The man with the *Wall Street Journal*
Thinks I am waiting for him
And comes up to me,
The invitation
For a double latte at Starbucks
Dying in his mouth
As he stares down at the ball of mucus and dirt
Curling back to life in my palm.

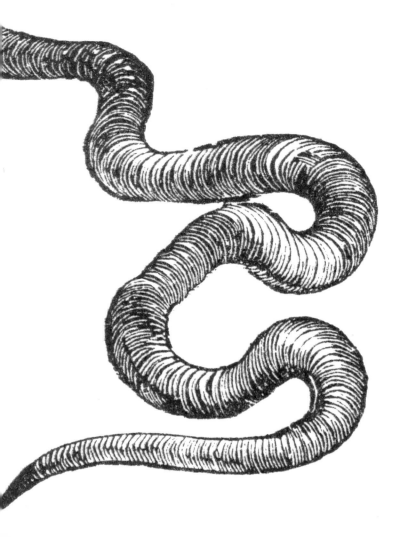

A Small Order
of Whimsy

RANTZ & NEELY
2003

Metaphysical Turmoil in the Termite Gut

ANTLER

Microorganisms in the intestines of termites
        are skeptical there's any outside world
                and put to death any microorganisms
        that have the audacity to suggest
                they live in the guts
of a wood-eating being
        or that such a thing as wood
even exists
        or that there are living beings
millions of times their size.
Meanwhile termites wander moon-luminous
        termite-mound corridors
                wondering where
        they and their loved ones go
                after they die.

Outside a Pink Stucco Apartment Building in South Central Los Angeles

CHERYL KLEIN

Lately spiders, ants and roaches
have stopped eating each other.
The cockroach carcass toppled
in the driveway,
its exoskeleton an appetizer
for feasting ants,
has been licked bare, eulogized.

Now the spiders, ants and roaches
hold meetings atop
webs fragile in structure,
irreplaceable in architecture.
They compare notes:

That motel at the top of
the Machu Picchu porch,
says a roach,
It's no four-star resort.
We lost Aunt Zeta last week.
The web swings with his weight
and lately
his friends have caught him watching
old episodes of *Batman* and swinging
his forewings like a leather cape.

Their host scratches her head
with one-eighth of her legs.
It appears our grocery store's
a war zone.
Comrades drowned down drains,
sucked up vacuums,
flattened by cat paws, Nike tread,
yesterday's headlines.
She has a cousin who lives inside
an iMac and reports back.

Yes, yes, echo the fire ants,
who look like beads on string.
Whose heads, close up, look like ripe dates
and who are thinking
the fire this time,
that it's not so much Darwin as Marx,
not so much Raid as songs
passed from antenna to antenna.

An Alphabetically Ordered Introduction to Our Contributors

PAT ANDRUS is a writing instructor at Bellevue Community College. She also has served as artist-in-residence for the state of Washington, as faculty for the Sitka Fine Arts Camp, and as an instructor for Elderhostel programs. Her poetry has been published both locally and nationally. Her letterpress chapbook *Daughter* appeared in 1987, and *Old Woman of Irish Blood*, an NEA-funded collection of her poetry, was published in 1997. She has produced, along with Northwest musician Mariana Van Blair and Texas writer Charles Dews, Celtic American poetry and Irish music through Beangan: The New Branch. Her other artistic endeavors include studying contemporary dance and movement, as well as collaborating with visual artists and videographers. She writes that she maintains "vital/life connections with earth's creatures." Her most recent summer residencies have been spent at Dorland Mountain Arts Colony, an artist retreat located on the nature preserve where she first encountered *Latrodectus hesperus*.

ANTLER, poet laureate of Milwaukee, is author of *Selected Poems* and other books. He has been the recipient of the Walt Whitman Award, a Pushcart Prize, and the Witter Bynner Prize from the American Academy and Institute of Arts and Letters in New York City. His work has been widely published, appearing in recent anthologies such as *Earth Prayers, Wild Songs: Poems from Wilderness, Practicing Deep Ecology, The Largeness the Small Is Capable Of, The Flutes of Power: Poetics of the Wild, The Soul Unearthed: Celebrating Wildness and Personal Renewal through Nature,* and *American Poets Say Goodbye to the 20th Century.* He writes that his "fascination with tiny beings was inspired by Kenneth Rexroth's epiphany—'Even the most ethereal vision of the mystic is knowledge much as an amoeba might be said to know of a man.' "

LYNNE BAMA lives in Wapiti, Wyoming, where she has worked as a writer, poet, and photographer for many years. Her work has appeared in *Orion, High Country News, Petroglyph,* and other publications. She recently received The Nature of Nature poetry prize from the Laura (Riding) Jackson Foundation of Sebastian, Florida. Her interest in harvester ants dates back to the late 1960s when she first flew over Wyoming and was "mystified" to find its open landscapes spotted with bare patches, "each with a bump in the center," and later realized that these odd features were ant mounds. She writes, "There are half a dozen colonies within 50 yards of our house. In spite of their bloodthirsty reputation, the ants seldom bite and have never caused any problems."

JOHN F. BARTHELL is associate professor of biology at the University of Central Oklahoma. He has authored many scientific articles, some of which appear in the western American journals *Southwestern Entomologist* and *Pan-Pacific Entomologist*, as well as in ecological journals such as *Ecological Applications*. His research interests include investigating the ways in which honey bees and nonnative solitary bees invade new environments through mutualistic interactions with nonnative plants. This specific interest has included collaborative work with the University of California and The Nature Conservancy on Santa Cruz Island, off the coast of southern California. Both he and his wife, Denise, a veterinarian, grew up in the western states of Wyoming and California. They live with their daughter, Kaitlyn, on a rural acreage outside Arcadia, Oklahoma, "alongside several 'blessed pets' that include cats, dogs, poultry, rabbits, and (of course) honey bees."

ELIZABETH BERNAYS grew up with a fascination for insects and flowers in the garden of her tropical Queensland home. After becoming an entomologist in England, she was involved in work related to insect pests in Africa and India before her appointment as professor at the University of California-Berkeley. A passion for grasshoppers brought her to the University of Arizona as head of Entomology, where she is currently Regents' Professor Emeritus. She continues her active research career, which includes publication of numerous scientific articles and books, but has "never ceased to be engaged by the aesthetics and evolutionary wonder of the most diverse group of animals on earth." In recent years she has turned to creative writing and has published several essays and poems in North American literary journals.

MELISSA BOROWICZ BETRUS has worked as a newspaper reporter and editor, jobs which allowed her to travel across the country. Originally from Buffalo, New York, she also has lived in Ketchikan, Alaska. She informs that, while always intrigued by the world's less appreciated creatures, yelling "Bug!" whenever she spotted one as a young child, it was in Alaska that she truly began to appreciate the natural world. Much of her free time there was spent hiking through and exploring the old-growth forests. Her appreciation for the outdoors has continued ever since, and she relishes the influence nature has on her life and on her work. Currently a graduate student in creative writing at Miami University and a writer/staff member for the university's alumni magazine *Miamian*, she lives with her husband in Oxford, Ohio.

FRED BROSSY is an organic farmer who is striving to create a more sustainable agriculture and to reduce his ecological footprint. For the last twenty years, he has been farming on the edge of Idaho's Snake River Plain along both sides of the Little Wood River a few miles west of the town of Shoshone. Among the diverse assortment of food and seed crops he grows, potatoes are a regular in the crop rotation and have provided him with many seasons of interaction with the Colorado potato beetle. He writes that, while his "relationship with this pesky arthropod has been frustrating at times over the years," he has "come to admire and respect the tenacity and adaptability of the beetle." Recently, as a complement to his lifelong journey as a farmer and student of the land, he has "returned to the halls of formal education" to pursue his undergraduate degree in agroecology from the Adult Degree Program at Prescott College in Arizona.

KELLY A. COFFMAN is an assistant kindergarten instructor at a small charter school. She writes that she celebrates her mornings "attempting to keep up with an inspiring pod of five-year-olds." Memories of her own early childhood are "speckled with arthropod encounters." She vividly recalls "sitting atop a fire ant hill and receiving dozens of painful reprimands, forming childhood friendships over that exhilarating summer evening ritual of catching and releasing lightning bugs, getting praised for accurate use of the family's (butterfly-shaped) fly-swatter while vacationing in 'Black Fly Point,' Michigan, and running a profitable business of removing fish flies off RVs in lakeside campgrounds for five cents apiece." She currently focuses her afternoon energies as a full-time student in the Adult Degree Program at Prescott College and "mulling over both the infinite wonders of the natural world and the deep wounds of our fragmented society." Her studies, she says, continue to lead her "towards the importance of returning to a conscious relationship with local place."

KIRBY CONGDON has authored many published collections of poetry over the last four decades. His books and chapbooks (including his ground-breaking writings on machines, comic-strip folklore, and erotic compulsion and violence in *Iron Ark, Juggernaut, Dream-Work,* and *Fantoccini*) reflect "the vulnerability of life and the lust for it in all its forms, natural and man-made." Three of his collections center on animals: *Cat Poems, Animals,* and "Fables," which he informs was "a cover story of 'modernized' versions of Aesop" written for the trilingual *Americas Magazine* (1966). He writes that his "arthropodic subjects include spiders, gnats, butterflies, moths, beach flies, horseshoe crabs, and an insect imbedded in amber, all of which prompt some form of empathy." His most recent collection is *"Novels": Prose Poems of People, Sixty-Five Years Ago, Old Mystic, Connecticut* (in press).

MARGARITA ENGLE is a botanist and the author of two critically acclaimed novels, *Singing to Cuba* and *Skywriting*. Her work has been widely anthologized and has appeared in literary journals in many countries and in several languages. She is the recipient of a San Diego Book Award, a Cintas Fellowship, as well as various short fiction, haiku, tanka, and poetry awards. Her most recent book is a collection of haiku, *Dreaming Sunlight*. She lives in central California with her husband, who is an entomologist, and her son and daughter.

CB FOLLETT, who received the 2001 National Poetry Book Award for *At the Turning of the Light,* writes that her poetry is "often about creatures of the air, earth, and water." She is "a daily watcher and saver of spiders, crane flies, wasps, beetles, and other creatures" and emphasizes that "no matter how small, they are each important companions." Her poetry has appeared in many journals and anthologies. She owns and operates Arctos Press and is publisher and coeditor of *Runes, A Review of Poetry.*

BOO HEISEY is a poet and writer, as well as a contributor to the 1997 Native West Press collection *Least Loved Beasts of the Really Wild West: A Tribute.* She writes, "As a youngster on my way home from school one rainy day, my relationship with nature began when I encountered a muster of snails forced from cover by the rain. My mother wasn't pleased when she opened the lunchbox

I had left on the kitchen counter to find it completely filled with the live escargot. From her reaction that day, I learned to respect wildlife from a distance and leave it in its place." She comments that, as a freelance writer, she has "time to reflect on the nature of things—including nature" and believes that "we should live off nature's interest, not her principal." She adds, "As to pests, I'm not convinced there are such things. A pest in one location is not necessarily a pest in another—everything in its place."

CAROL N. KANTER is a widely published poet and a psychotherapist with a private practice. After completing undergraduate work in biology, she earned a master's degree in clinical social work and a doctorate in counseling psychology. Her poems have appeared in many anthologies and literary journals including *Iowa Woman, Kaleidoscope Ink, Blue Unicorn, ByLine, Explorations, Rambunctious Review, River Oak Review, The Madison Review, The Mid-America Poetry Review,* and others. Her honors include Illinois winner of *Korone's* 2001 writing project, an International Merit Award in poetry from the *Atlanta Review* (1998), and first prize in Poets and Patrons' International Narrative Poetry Contest (1995). Her book *And Baby Makes Three* explores the emotional transition to parenthood. She sees "all life as sharing a kinship" and often finds that other species show up in her poetry. She and her husband live in Evanston, Illinois, and are parents of two daughters.

STEPHEN R. KELLERT is Tweedy Ordway Professor of Social Ecology at the Yale University School of Forestry and Environmental Studies. His pioneering work for over two decades involved exploring public perceptions and attitudes related to nature, including species preference, and developing a comprehensive values typology for the concept of biophilia. His current work focuses on understanding the connection between human and natural systems, with an emphasis on the value and conservation of nature, as well as on designing ways to harmonize the natural and human-built environments. Included among his many awards are the National Conservation Achievement Award (National Wildlife Federation) and the Distinguished Individual Achievement Award (Society for Conservation Biology). His books *Kinship to Mastery: Biophilia in Human Evolution and Development* and *The Value of Life: Biological Diversity and Human Society* are two of his numerous publications.

He also has served as coeditor for a number of books, including the following: *The Good in Nature and Humanity: Connecting Science, Religion, and Spirituality with the Natural World* (with T. Farnham); *Children and Nature: Psychological, Sociocultural, and Evolutionary Investigations* (with P. Kahn, Jr.); and *The Biophilia Hypothesis* (with E. O. Wilson). His latest book, *Ordinary Nature: Understanding and Designing Natural Process in Everyday Life,* is currently in press.

CHERYL KLEIN received her undergraduate degree in English from the University of California-Los Angeles and her MFA in critical studies from California Institute of the Arts. Her writing has appeared in *Doorknobs & Bodypaint, Delirium Journal, Blithe House Quarterly,* and *CrossConnect.* She works in the California office of Poets & Writers, Inc., a nonprofit literary organization. She lives in Los Angeles, where she attempts "to avoid hurting insects and spiders," although her cats, she writes, "often indulge their hunting instincts." She has been a champion of maligned animals since age 16 when she wrote a poem protesting the persecution of pigeons.

JOANNE E. LAUCK is an environmental educator and author of the widely acclaimed book *The Voice of the Infinite in the Small: Re-Visioning the Insect-Human Connection.* She holds a master's degree in psychology, and her writing consistently addresses the healing potential of the human-animal bond. It was while researching the transformative power of interactions between people and animals many years ago that the insect-human connection came to the forefront for her. She says, "I've been working for the insects ever since." By taking a psychological and spiritual view of our relationship to insects, her intention is "to reveal the blind spot in our culture that has put us on the battlefield with them." Her work showcases insects as "the messengers that they are—in the environment and as emissaries of the divine." In addition, she works with at-risk teens and young adults, providing non-traditional support and mentoring through her nonprofit organization, Catalyst for Youth, Inc. She writes, "We need to enlarge our circle of community to include both insects and youth. Both groups are on the receiving end of fear-based projections and desperately need our good attention and blessing."

SARA LITTLECROW-RUSSELL is Anishinaabe-Han Metís, a single mother of two, an activist, and a Public Interest Law Fellow at Northeastern School of Law in Boston. Her award-winning poetry and articles have been published in a wide variety of magazines, journals, and anthologies. Poems in her manuscript "Eagle Feathers across a Crow Wing" have been published in a variety of journals including *The Massachusetts Review, American Indian Quarterly, Race Traitor, Flyaway, Red Ink, U.S. Latino Review, Femspec, Survivor, AIM Magazine,* and *Hip Mama.* Her poems are anthologized in many books including *Sister Nations: Native American Women Writing on Community,* the erotic anthology *Touched by Eros,* and in Winona LaDuke's book, *All Our Relations: Native Struggles for Land and Life.* In regard to those she refers to as "insect relatives," she writes that "like indigenous peoples, insects are too often marginalized as invisible and expendable; in reality they are both integral to the balance of life. To honor an insect is to honor the foundational sacredness of this balance."

JEFFREY A. LOCKWOOD is a professor of entomology at the University of Wyoming. He has studied rangeland grasshoppers for 17 years, and his book *Grasshopper Dreaming,* a collection of essays, reflects his struggle with killing the creatures that he has come to love. He recently received a John Burroughs Award of Recognition for his essay "Voices from the Past," which chronicles the life and sudden disappearance of the irruptive populations of locusts, including single swarms 1,800 miles long and 110 miles wide, that devastated pioneer settlements in the 1870s and 1880s. In addition, he is a recent recipient of a Pushcart Prize for his essay "To Be Honest," a memoir of his spiritual, ethical, and intellectual struggles to make sense of being a "hired assassin" for agriculture. Both award-winning essays first appeared in *Orion.* His professional associations, he comments, reflect his "understanding of grasshoppers as 'blessed pests.'" He is the executive director of the Orthopterists Society (a worldwide scientific organization dedicated to the study of grasshoppers, locusts, crickets, and katydids), the director of the Association for Applied Acridology International (the first and only humanitarian-based NGO of entomologists in the world devoted to assisting people in sustainable management of grasshoppers and locusts), and a member of the editorial board of the *Journal of Insect Conservation.*

LOU MASSON is a professor at the University of Portland where for many years he has taught courses on the literature of nature and the out-of-doors. He writes that as a boy growing up in the Berkshire Hills, he "tried to catch insects in a net," but now he tries "to capture them in poems." He is author of the published collection *Reflections: Essays on Place and Family*. Most recently his stories and poems have appeared in such journals and magazines as *StringTown, Calapooya, Real, Ekphrasis, Portland, Footsteps, Off the Coast,* and *National Catholic Reporter.*

JANE MAYES is a retired high school librarian who pens a weekly newspaper column, "Lit., etc." Author of two poetry chapbooks, *Impressions* and *Scene to Unseen*, she writes that she has been attracted to fauna and flora since her childhood, "keeping count of wildlife sightings on trips and tramping around creeks and woods of Michigan." She comments that while she feels "favored when an attractive insect lands" on her, she admits to being "repelled by wasps and earwigs." A mother of three children and grandmother of six, she enjoys biking, swimming, kayaking, gardening, golfing, and painting with watercolors. She and her husband live on the shore of Lake Huron at Port Austin, Michigan, where they raise Standardbred horses.

PHILIP MILLER is a poet whose work for many years has appeared in a wide variety of literary forums. He has authored three books of poetry, *Cats in the House, Hard Freeze,* and *From the Temperate Zone* (with Keith Denniston), as well as a number of chapbooks, including *Father's Day* (1995 Winner of the Ledge Press chapbook contest). His fourth book, *Branches Snapping,* and another chapbook, *Grandma Rose,* are both forthcoming. His poetry has been published in numerous journals such as *Poetry, Rattapallax, Georgia Review,* and *Chelsea.* He writes, "I have always loved insects, I think, ever since I watched my father, Richard Miller, drawing and painting them and capturing their strange and beautiful shapes and colors."

TIM MYERS is a writer, songwriter, and storyteller who also teaches at Santa Clara University in the Bay Area. His *Basho and the Fox* was read on NPR, made the *New York Times* bestseller list for children's works, and was a *Smithsonian* Notable Children's Book, as well as a Children's Book Council "Not Just for Children Anymore" selection. He has authored many pieces in major children's magazines and has three new children's books coming out. He is also a widely published poet with a chapbook currently in press. Other honors related to his creative endeavors include winning a national poetry contest judged by John Updike and receiving a prize in an international contest for speculative fiction. Although he admits to "moments of entomophobia," he expresses that he was "utterly taken by the beauty of the katydid" he wrote about for this anthology and further comments that he thereby understands "that much more the beauty of the American West."

KEVIN M. O'NEILL is professor of entomology at Montana State University in Bozeman, where he teaches courses in entomology, evolution, and animal behavior. In addition to his books *The Natural History and Behavior of North American Beewolves* (with Howard Evans) and *Solitary Wasps: Natural History and Behavior*, he has authored many published scientific papers on insect behavior and ecology. He comments that "this is all somewhat surprising" because he "hated insects as a kid and expected to grow up to be an ornithologist, history teacher, or Hall-of-Fame centerfielder (or maybe all three)." But he became an entomologist, he says, "after undergraduate courses in entomology led to the lucky accident of studying in graduate school under Howard Ensign Evans, one of the world's great entomophiles." He writes that he is "still a birdwatcher, an avid reader of history, and a centerfielder on a second-rate softball team." He and his wife, Ruth, also an entomologist, live with their two sons, Samuel and Thomas, in Bozeman.

KENNETH POBO is author of two recent collections of poetry, *Introductions* (in press) and *Ordering: A Season in My Garden*. He expresses that he feels connected to bugs, especially through gardening. He also likes spiders and wishes that "many politicians would fall into their webs to be their dinners" (though he asks the spiders "to forgive the indigestion"). He especially enjoys the northwoods of Wisconsin, "a buggy world," particularly from June through September. He writes that "bugs, frogs, herons, and people form a mosaic" into which he "grudgingly" admits gnats. His poetry has appeared over many years in numerous literary journals, some of which include *Nimrod, Oklahoma Review, Hawaii*

Review, Pacific Review, Colorado Review, Atlanta Review, The Fiddlehead, Mudfish, Apalachee Quarterly, and many other publications.

JEFF PONIEWAZ is author of *Dolphin Leaping in the Milky Way,* for which he received a Discovery Award from the international writers' organization PEN. He teaches his "Literature of Ecological Vision" course at the University of Wisconsin-Milwaukee. Over the years, he has taught and performed at the Kerouac Poetics School in Boulder and has given presentations on Cetacean Consciousness at the New College in San Francisco and on Poetry of Wilderness at Esalen Institute in Big Sur. He writes that his "eco-activism spans from local urban greenspace preservation to the global rainforest catastrophe." His creative work, including his environmental poetry, extends across several decades and has been widely published in a diversity of anthologies, journals, and forums such as the *Los Angeles Times, Greenpeace Chronicles, Earth First!, New York Quarterly, Beloit Poetry Journal, The World, Minnesota Review, The Wisconsin Poets Calendar,* and others. His last name (pronounced Poe-nYEAH-vAHsh), he informs, is Polish for "Because."

ROBERT MICHAEL PYLE is internationally known for fathering the now widely quoted concept of "the extinction of experience." He is author of many award-winning books, including *Wintergreen, The Thunder Tree, Where Bigfoot Walks, Chasing Monarchs, Walking the High Ridge,* and several standard butterfly books. He writes that he "switched from seashells to butterflies at the age of eleven" when it became apparent that his native Colorado offered more scope for the latter. He received his doctorate in ecology and environmental studies from Yale University in 1976, has worked as Northwest Land Steward for The Nature Conservancy, and has consulted in giant birdwing butterfly management in Papua New Guinea. In addition, he founded the Xerces Society for invertebrate conservation. He has been the recipient of numerous honors and awards, some of which include a Distinguished Service Award from the Society for Conservation Biology, a John Burroughs Medal, a Guggenheim Fellowship, and many others. An independent writer, he lives along a tributary of the Lower Columbia River and speaks, reads, and teaches widely in forums such as universities, literary festivals, and natural-history field courses.

ELISAVIETTA RITCHIE is a widely published, award-winning author and poet who writes that she "would have been a biologist" had she mastered math. Currently residing in both Washington, D.C., and Broomes Island, Maryland, she teaches creative writing workshops for adults and serves as a poet-in-the-schools. Included among her many books are *In Haste I Write You This Note: Stories and Half-Stories* (co-winner of Washington Writers' Publishing House Award, 2000); *Flying Time: Stories and Half-Stories* (which includes four PEN Syndicated Fiction winners); *The Arc of the Storm*; *Elegy for the Other Woman: New and Selected Terribly Female Poems*; *Tightening the Circle Over Eel Country* (winner of Great Lakes Colleges Association's New Writer's Award, 1975-76); *Raking the Snow* (winner of the Washington Writers' Publishing House competition, 1981-82); *Timbot*; and *Wild Garlic: The Journal of Maria X*. In addition to authoring many published collections, she is editor of the book *The Dolphin's Arc: Endangered Creatures of the Sea*. Her manuscript "Awaiting Permission to Land" received the 2001 Anamnesis Poetry Award. She writes that "all creatures except wasps have found a certain if sometimes brief welcome" into her home, poems, and stories.

HARLEY G. SHAW is author of *Soul among Lions: The Cougar as Peaceful Adversary*, as well as numerous articles in scientific journals and wildlife magazines. He worked as a research biologist for the Arizona Game and Fish Department for 27 years. At that time, most of his research centered on population studies of puma and Merriam's wild turkey. He writes that, while he was born and spent most of his life in Arizona, he "abandoned" his home state "when humans became more abundant than jackrabbits." He refers to himself as a "devoted misanthrope" who avoided living in towns with stoplights for 35 years. He now lives in "an empty county" in New Mexico with only one stoplight—40 miles from his home— and says that he considers "scorpions, coyotes, Gila monsters, rattlesnakes, packrats, and cone-nosed bugs to be better neighbors than all Republicans and most Democrats." He is currently writing a history of the absence and presence of juniper within regions north of Prescott, Arizona.

JOHN SULLIVAN earned his MFA in creative writing from the University of Illinois at Chicago. He writes that he has held a number of jobs "in the Windy City," including warehouseman, mail handler, and laborer. He is currently a night watchman who, during his hours on the graveyard shift, occasionally finds himself "admiring the arthropods—spiders, millipedes, pill bugs, moths, crane flies, crickets, and the like—for their adaptability, ingenuity, and pluck." He points out that "inspirational speakers stress the need to alter habits, let go of the past, and change," adding, "What better examples of successful change than these marvelous, diversified creatures." His poetry is forthcoming in *Confrontation*, *South Carolina Review*, and *Whiskey Island Magazine*.

JAY UDALL is author of three books of poetry, the most recent being *Home in the Dark*. His poems, as well as short stories, have appeared in many publications. He writes that he "developed close associations with fireflies, water striders, mosquitoes, and wolf spiders" when growing up in Virginia; however, he credits "the Japanese haiku master Issa (1763-1827) with showing the possibilities of honoring our insect brethren in poetry." He lives with his wife, Suzanne, and daughter, Rachel Lee, in Santa Fe, New Mexico, where he serves as office manager and legal assistant for the Navajo Uranium Miners and Widows Fund.

CHRISTINE VALENTINE settled in Montana after coming to this country from England in 1964. When in the United Kingdom she had been pursuing a degree in biology, but she changed majors upon coming to the United States, graduating with a degree in human services from Chief Dull Knife College in Lame Deer, Montana. She has worked for the Northern Cheyenne Tribe for twenty-five years. She writes, "When I came to Montana, I did not realize the amazing number of insects that live in our area," informing that common insects are crickets, moths, small centipedes, and many beetles. She also observes a large variety of spiders. In regard to both insects and spiders, she says, "These creatures are important to the natural order in our world; I prefer to live with them or relocate them, rather than to kill them."

DIANALEE VELIE is an award-winning poet, author, and playwright. Her poems have appeared in hundreds of journals worldwide, most recently in the *Connecticut River Review* and *Peregrine*. Her short stories have also appeared in numerous anthologies.

She conducts poetry workshops throughout the country and has taught poetry and writing at the State University of New York-Purchase, Manhattanville College, Norwalk Community College, the University of Connecticut, the ILEAD program at Dartmouth, the College for Life Long Learning and the Adventures in Learning program at Colby-Sawyer College. She is a passionate poet and writer who engages her readers and students, constantly challenging them to own their unique voices. She holds an undergraduate degree from Sarah Lawrence College and a master's degree in writing from Manhattanville College, where she also served as editor of *Inkwell Magazine*. She notes that she is "unable to step on an ant," preferring instead "to leave a trail of honey leading them outdoors."

PATRICIA M. WOODRUFF is a writer, community activist, and backyard naturalist. The incident by which she marks her moment of "discovering the magic of the biological world" came when she was about nine. On her way to get the afternoon paper, she heard the sound of a kitten mewing from the direction of a small, willowy creek. She knew that her family "could not have small pets because of allergies," but she was determined to find the kitten, anyway. She searched and struggled through the brush, but all she saw was "a small gray bird with a bright orange patch under its tail, and so distinct" that she "dropped the search for the kitten and went to look up the bird in the *Little Golden Book of Birds*." She discovered what she now refers to as her "first bird"—the catbird. She remarks that this discovery fueled a curiosity and an appreciation of the richness of the natural world that enriched her life through many moves around the United States. She chose a career in natural resources, becoming "the first Natural Area Coordinator at Arizona State Parks," adding that "after a few unproductive years in government," she founded a small publishing business. She says that she intends to continue discovering the West.

ALLEN M. YOUNG is curator of zoology and vice president of collections, research, and public programs at the Milwaukee Public Museum. He is author of numerous scientific articles and several books on insect natural history and ecology, his field of scientific expertise. In addition, he has written essays and commentaries on this subject for popular venues such as the *Chicago Tribune, New*

York Times, Wall Street Journal, and a variety of magazines. One of his most recent books, *Small Creatures and Ordinary Places,* a collection of seasonal essays on insects and other small animals, won the Ellis/Henderson Outdoor Writing Award from the Council of Wisconsin Writers. A recently elected Fellow of the Wisconsin Academy of Sciences, Arts and Letters, he has devoted much of his life not only to research on insects, but also to enhancing public understanding of the central role that insects play in the overall design of life. His interest in insects began when he was a child growing up in New York and rearing native silk moths and butterflies. Among his many projects reflective of his lifework has been the preparation of a revised edition of the *Golden Guide to Insects,* an earlier edition of which inspired his boyhood fascination with the life cycles of insects.

NATIVE WEST PRESS

Native West Press is a small press in Prescott, Arizona, with a special emphasis on indigenous wildlife and the natural history of the American West. NWP is dedicated to enhancing public awareness of the importance of *natural* biodiversity, particularly within the western regions of the United States. The press was founded in 1996 by Yvette A. Schnoeker-Shorb and Terril L. Shorb.

Also from NATIVE WEST PRESS ...

Javelina Place: The Controversial Face of the Collared Peccary

Edited by Yvette A. Schnoeker-Shorb and Terril L. Shorb

$7.95 plus $1.50 for shipping and handling ($7.95 plus $3.00 for Priority Mail)

Least Loved Beasts of the Really Wild West: A Tribute

Edited by Terril L. Shorb and Yvette A. Schnoeker-Shorb

$8.95 plus $1.50 for shipping and handling ($8.95 plus $3.00 for Priority Mail)

The Spiders and Spirits of Petunia Manor

By Yvette A. Schnoeker-Shorb and Terril L. Shorb

$6.95 plus $1.50 for shipping and handling ($6.95 plus $3.00 for Priority Mail)

For more information or to order these books:

Native West Press
P.O. Box 12227
Prescott, AZ 86304
e-mail: nativewestpres@cableone.net
www.nativewestpress.com

144